2009 Poetry Com

I have a dream 2009
Words to change the world

Martin Luther King

John Lennon

Southern Poets
Edited by Helen Davies

First published in Great Britain in 2009 by:

Young Writers
Remus House
Coltsfoot Drive
Peterborough
PE2 9JX
Telephone: 01733 890066
Website: www.youngwriters.co.uk

All Rights Reserved
Book Design by Spencer Hart & Tim Christian
© Copyright Contributors 2009
SB ISBN 978-1-84924-391-9

Foreword

'I Have a Dream 2009' is a series of poetry collections written by 11 to 18-year-olds from schools and colleges across the UK and overseas. Pupils were invited to send us their poems using the theme 'I Have a Dream'. Selected entries range from dreams they've experienced to childhood fantasies of stardom and wealth, through inspirational poems of their dreams for a better future and of people who have influenced and inspired their lives.

The series is a snapshot of who and what inspires, influences and enthuses young adults of today. It shows an insight into their hopes, dreams and aspirations of the future and displays how their dreams are an escape from the pressures of today's modern life. Young Writers are proud to present this anthology, which is truly inspired and sure to be an inspiration to all who read it.

Contents

Featherstone High School, Southall
Harinder Ahluwalia (13) ... 1

Herschel Grammar School, Slough
Rupinder Hanspal (12) ... 2
Maleeha Masood (11) ... 3
Aman Grover (13) ... 4
Devisha Raithatha (13) ... 5
Mehreen Khan (12) ... 6
Jai Hodgson (13) ... 7
Sarah Ghani (13) ... 8
Amrita Atwal (12) ... 9
Joanne Hayati (13) ... 10
Satyam Vora (12) ... 11
Afoo Khan (13) ... 12
Amy Tough (13) ... 12
Aneesah Mughal (12) ... 13
Talha Sabir (12) ... 14
Jamie Woodman (12) ... 15
Yash Karia (15) ... 16
Shivali Jain (10) ... 17
Robyn Campbell (12) ... 18
Claudia Silva (12) ... 19
Anagha Sharma (11) ... 20
Liam Addley (13) ... 20
Anushka Jagpal (11) ... 21
Jananan Krishnanandan (11) ... 21
Sophia Ahmad (11) ... 22
Hannah James (13) ... 23
Natalie Morrison (13) ... 24
Sandeep Singh (12) ... 25
Sam Rowell (11) ... 26
Sam Cheema (13) ... 27
Sameer Moghal (11) ... 28
Lily Smart (13) ... 28
Amar Hack (11) ... 29
Moaiz Malik (12) ... 29
Asad Ahmed (12) ... 30
Tarnjot Virdee (11) ... 31
Aditya Arjun (12) ... 31
Manveet Dhaliwal (13) ... 32

Kate Horwell (12) ... 32
Hassam Kashmiri ... 33
Jack Porter (12) ... 33

Hertswood Lower School, Borehamwood
Jodie Reilly (13) ... 34
Simeon Nichols (14) ... 35
Ratidzo Masunda (13) ... 36
Molly McDonagh (14) ... 37
Ben Molyneux (14) ... 38
Chloe Hayes (11) ... 38
Callan Jones (11) ... 39
Jack McMaster (12) ... 39
Annique Debeauville (14) ... 40
Jordan Saville (11) ... 40
Chloe Livermore (12) ... 41
Connie O'Connell (12) ... 41
Shannon Kane (12) ... 42
Adrian Bernstein (12) ... 42
Emmanuel Banjo (14) ... 43
Cara Elvins ... 43
Tae Kyung Baek (12) ... 44
Samantha Lewis (12) ... 44
Louise Munting (12) ... 45
Lucy Starnes, Nicole Antonio
& Billie Hampson (13) ... 45
Mink Goodman (14) ... 46
Jack McWilliam (14) ... 46
Chase Rochester (12) ... 47
Tom McConnon-Evans
& Scott Lindsey (13) ... 47
Sam Prangnell (12) ... 48
Annabelle Lisowski (11) ... 48
Charlie Bowsher (12) ... 49
Frank Harrison (14) ... 49
Shannon Hurley (12) ... 50
Jade Anne Perry (12) ... 50
Chris Gee (11) ... 51
Paige McClintock (11) ... 51
Ellen Carrick (12) ... 52

Ben Larter (11) 52
Chelsea Pritchard (12) 52
Jake Blyth (11) 53

JFS School, Kenton
Jade Clapich (14) 53
Elinor Roth (14) 54
Ella Landsman (14) 56
Chloe Rich (14) 57
Matt Polden (14) 58
Nivi Kanel (13) 59
Georgia Lubert (14) 60
Sebastian Tuckman (14) 61
Boaz Goldwater (14) 62
Elie Kraft (13) 63
Dan Hadary (13) 64
Georgia Bass (13) 65
Daniel Sugarman (14) 66
Charles Langsford (14) 67
Gabrielle Abadi (14) 67
Yuval Cohen (13) & Soheil Assil (14) 68
Adam Childs (13) 68
Laura Imzayin (14) 69
Elliott Scott (14) 70

Kingham Hill School, Chipping Norton
Katie Dawson (13) 70
Alice Hilborn (13) 71
Sophie Laing (12) 72
Leya Womersley (13) 73
Joshua Goddard (13) 74

Margaret Beaufort Middle School, Riseley
Simon Dyer (13) 74
Alastair Declan Sparham (13) 75
Alex Pinfold (12) 76
Ryan Bullock (13) 77
Olivia Jackson (12) 78
Molly Nicholls (12) 78
Charlotte Furneaux (13) 79
Emily May (12) 79
Max Taylor 80
Elsie Sturton (11) 80
Tim Palmer (13) 81

Liam Beckwith & Jordan Nicholson (13) . 81
Jack Hunter (12) & Dean Watson (13) ... 82
Laura Regan (13) 82
Olivia Francis (12) 83
Lizzie Moor (12) 83
Bryanna Harding (12) 84
Jordan Johnston (11) 84
Liam Henderson (13) 85
Polly Witherick (11) 85
Nathan Tennant (11) 86
Jack Johnson (12) 86
Sappho Holland (12) 87
Emily Woodhead (12) 87
Gemma Fensham (12) 88
Tia Carroll (13) 88
Alexander Dimmock (12) 89
Francesca Graham (11) 89
Gemma Woodhead (11) 90
Becky Telling (12) 90
Mark Willey (13) 91
Natasha Fensome (11) 91
Mark Cooper (12) 92
Tom Walton (12) 92
Louis Gibson (12) 93
Olivia Smith (12) 93
Arpan Sekhon (13) 94
Daniel Spiers (13) 94
Eden Crawley (13) 95
Peter Feneley (12) 95
Lucy Bates (12) 96
Gabrielle Kyreacou (11) 96
Ben Hoogstraten (12) 97
Anya Luka-Langley (12) 97
Oliver Stokoe (12) 97
Kitty Rowland (11) 98
Ollie King (11) 98
Tilly Rubens (12) 99
Jade Barnes (12) 99
Zach Witherick (11) 99
Jonathan Hargreaves (12) ... 100

Moyles Court School, Ringwood
Amy Henry (15) 100
Kim Chung (14) 101
Alex Parkinson (12) 102

Emily Cooke (15)	103
Anna Patterson (11)	104
Alice Clark (15)	105
Douglas Murdoch (13)	106
Lauren Palmer (11)	107
Anna Peachey (16)	108
Khlöe Smith (12)	109
Jasmine Kingsley-Cole (11)	110
Meredith Jones (13)	111
Charlotte Eldon (10)	112
Danny Whitelock (15)	113
Spencer Jones (11)	113
Jasmine West (11)	114
Becky Brown (16)	115
Zahra Hall (11)	115
Megan Victoria Price (16)	116
Alex Wood (11)	116
Luke Stevens (14)	117
Christopher Winrow (16)	118
Josh Cummings (14)	118
Aly Davie (12)	119
Sam Wilkes (13)	119
Charlotte Barna (16)	120
Henry Glaister (14)	120
Rosie Lees (15)	121
Diggory Simons (13)	121
Jack Wilson (12)	122
Olivia Argent (10)	122
Mikey Kingsley (13)	123
Rosie Kerr (15)	123
Tom Brown (11)	124
Robert Fraser (15)	124
Jade Metcalfe (15)	125
Florence Radford (11)	125
Lauren Wright (13)	126
Lloyd Geddis (12)	126
Rachel Lucas (15)	127
Scott Jones (14)	127
Jade Sax (15)	128

Northolt High School, Northolt

Amyna Visram (14)	128
Athena Echave (13)	129
Janany Sathasivam (14)	130
Daniel Ewusie-Wilson (13)	131

James Kilduff (14)	132
Gowry Ganenthira (13)	133
Siham Ali (15)	134
Kimberley Seaward (14)	135
Ryan Butler (14)	135
James Ellett (14)	136
Jamie Carpenter (13)	136
Katie Conroy (13)	137
Charlotte Davies (13)	137
Ikram Abdulle (14)	138
Max Petty (13)	138
Alanna Clarke-Beattie (14)	139
Jake Holmyard (14)	139
Paige Tyson-Simmons (13)	140
Holly Lane (14)	140
Steven Harding (13)	141
Risha Basit (14)	141
Martyn Thomas (13)	142

Oxted School, Oxted

Bessie Ephgrave (12)	142
Lauren Faulkner (12)	143
Bethany Arnell (12)	144
Sophie Conquest (12)	145
Luke Thompson (12)	145
Jessica Muscio (12)	146
Molly Cook (12)	146
Sophie Potter (12)	147
Genevieve Hadida	147
Dylan Middleton (11)	148
Tom Thornley (13)	148
Eleanor Harber	149
Sam Carpenter (13)	149

Selsdon High School, Croydon

Emma Felton (13)	150
Magdalina Strumelieva (13)	151
Imanna Kirby (13)	152
Courtney Bain (14)	153
Paul Dawkins (12)	154
Nathasha Berry (13)	155
Clay Pel-Is (13)	155
Cindy Okech (13)	156
Reece Wright (11)	156
Sadia Kubie (13)	157

Abel Kinganga (14) 157
Tarnya Grover (14) 158
Edgar Morais (13) 158
Yasmin Allwood (14) 159

The Cottesloe School, Leighton Buzzard

Holly McCarthy (14) 159
Adreen Hart-Rule (17) 160
Will Guyon (14) 161
Scarlett Miles (13) 162
Yasmin Chambers (14) 163
Harry McCartney (13) 164
Heather Potton (13) 165
Eddie Wiggins (14) 166
Alice Berry (14) 167
Shannan Mitchener (14) 168
Alfie Gardner-Potter (13) 169
George Langston (14) 170
Beth Styles (14) 171
Rodney Peters (14) 171
Sammie Joanne Wootten (14) 172
Zara Ashton (13) 173
Chris Worlock (13) 173
Emma Whittome (14) 174
Tom Herbert (14) 174
Chloe Brown (14) 175
Ben Cleaver (13) 175

The Douay Martyrs School, Ickenham

James Reynolds (17) 176
Ashik Santimon (15) 177
Mark Migallos (14) 178
Andy Luu (15) 179
Katherine Hourihan (13) 180
Kirsty Brown (16) 181
Sherree Rosario (16) 182
Sasha Garrett (14) 183
Charlotte Mitchell (13) 184
Joseph McDonnell (13) 185
Sean Donnelly (16) 186
Natalie Potts (13) 187
Naeem Dowlut (14) 188
Arjan Singh Lall (13) 189

Helen Jones (13) 190
Jack Haynes (16) 191
Samantha Chigbo (14) 192
Anna Alvarez (14) 192
Alice Connolly (12) 193
Tara Swann (14) 193
Roisin Callanan (16) 194
Natasha Landy (15) 195
Risa Quadros (15) 195
Megan Halligan (15) 196
Bethan Notley-Jones (13) 197
Milen Ghebremichael (13) 198
Stephanie Beaver (16) 199
Katy Little (16) 200
Derwinne Carlos (15) 200
Betsi Burch (13) 201
Pooja Sharma (14) 201
Amisha Raniga (16) 202
James Hester (15) 203
Megan Finch (13) 204
Hannah Eddery (15) 205
Mia Evans (13) 206
Roshni Solanki (13) 206
James Griffin (17) 207
Patrick Nash (13) 207
Amber Goonesekera (14) 208
Daniel Haras-Gummer (15) 208

The Poems

I Have A Dream 2009 - Southern Poets

Child's Cry

Ever heard a child cry out in pain
Screaming, 'Stop Daddy, it hurts!'?
Her delicate little face scrunched up in vain
Little does she know that he's hooked on drugs.

Her mother comes back from work
As soon as she sees her daughter
She bursts into tears, 'What happened to you?' she asks
But Susan just stares into her loving face.

'Nick, Nick! What has happened to Susan?' she asks
'Nothing, darling, she's fine, why what has happened?'
'Someone has almost killed her,' she cries
Behind that innocent face, Nick's the one to blame.

Nee-noo-nee-noo!
The police are over in ten minutes flat
Questioning who, what, when, where and why?
Searching the house for evidence
Under the sofa they find drugs.

'Why?' she screams
'How could you? I trusted you.'
Susan just cries into her mother's arms
Whilst her mother cries at her father.

Nick is sentenced for fifteen years,
Whilst mother and daughter mend their lives.
Everybody giving support,
Praying to God with hope that this doesn't happen to anyone else.

Harinder Ahluwalia (13)
Featherstone High School, Southall

Dream

Dream
That you have a hundred diamonds beside you
Dream
You are going down a waterslide shouting, *'Woohoo!'*
Dream
You have a day to play with mates
Dream
School starts very late
Dream
You go to Spain for ten weeks
Dream
Your answers are ahead of you and you get to have a peek
Dream
The Credit Crunch never came around
Dream
That you have £6,000,000
Dream
You have a fun job
Dream
Your name is Bob
Dream
You are a monkey
Dream
The 1900s were funky
Dream
That you are never very sad
Dream
You become a mum or a dad
Dream
There were never African slaves
Dream
The Americans will, one day, behave

Dream
Racism stops
Dream
Your door of dreams is never locked.
Dream!

Rupinder Hanspal (12)
Herschel Grammar School, Slough

I Have A Dream . . .

I have a dream that one day all wars will end
and people will be able to sit together
without the heat of hatred between them.

I have a dream that one day poor will be poor no more
and will be able to sit and dine like the rich.

I have a dream that one day everyone will bend down
and pick up a piece of rubbish and put it in the bin
so we will be able to live in a healthy environment.

I have a dream that one day we will live our lives with no restrictions.

I have a dream that one day different people will be able to walk
down the streets without being a victim of racism.

I have a dream that one day people will be able to live safely
and there will be no crime.

I have a dream that one day whoever has done a bad deed
will be forgiven and will have the chance to start again.

I have a dream that one day people will judge you not by the colour
of your skin or what you look like, but by your personality.

I have a dream that one day children will be allowed to run free
in their own country without meeting soldiers
who have invaded their land.

I have a dream that one day the sun will rise again
and all will be peaceful and all will have dreams and hopes
to look up to.

Maleeha Masood (11)
Herschel Grammar School, Slough

I'm Going To Paint A Perfect Picture

I have a dream
That my fingers will scrape and twirl and shade
And I will create the perfect picture
The perfect picture of a perfect world

I have a dream
That at the top of my picture
The painted ancestors will look down and smile
At the clear blue skies and unpolluted streams

I have a dream
That the little carved men and women
Need not judge each other by the colour of their skin
Let it be black, white, cream or blue

I have a dream
That my outlined soldiers put down their guns
And stretch out their hands
However strange it may be

I have a dream
That my shaded land
Shall not be touched by bombs and grenades
But by footprints and handprints

I have a dream
That my coloured animals
Can swing and gallop to their hearts' content
Without ending up in yesterday's stew

I have a dream
That my paintbrush and pencil
Will create a world so perfect
It will be a perfect world

I have a dream
That my grandchildren will find my painting and say,
'Doesn't this look familiar?'
That day I will know . . .
My picture is perfect in every way.

Aman Grover (13)
Herschel Grammar School, Slough

A Different World

A different world
In my mind,
A different place
In my dreams,
Lots of colours.

White for unity,
To bring mankind together,
White for serenity,
Peace with others forever.

Blue for water,
Having enough every day
Blue for the sky,
So the clouds don't turn grey.

Yellow for the sun,
To make our crops grow,
Yellow for happiness,
To make our faces glow.

Green for the environment,
To keep it safe and alive,
Green is for nature
To help it grow and thrive.

Red is for warmth,
For energy, for joy
Red is for our world
Which we must not destroy

A different world
In my mind,
A different place
In my dreams,
Lots of colours.

Devisha Raithatha (13)
Herschel Grammar School, Slough

I Too Have A Dream

I too have a dream.

I have a dream that people will be able
To live their lives in happiness,
Not the misery many are trapped in,
And celebrate who they are,
Amidst encouragement,
Not rejection.

I dream that people will break free
Of the chains of hate
And help build a world brimming with
Peace and prosperity.

I too have a dream.

I have a dream that our differences,
Whether small or big,
Will be treated as our individuality
And give a chance in our world
For those who don't have one.

I dream that in the days after this one,
The smile of equality will be seen on every man,
Woman
And child, regardless of the colour of their skin.

I too have a dream.

I dream that some day,
The struggle will be over,
That there will be a right and wrong
And the sun will rise
To a world of equality, peace and unity.

I too have a dream.

Mehreen Khan (12)
Herschel Grammar School, Slough

Baby Dreams

Have you ever wondered
What a baby dreams?
A tiny newborn baby
Of what does it dream?
It dreams of happy
Never sad
Always good
Never bad
It dreams of rich
Never poor
Never less
Always more
It dreams of the perfect world
Imagine if its dreams unfurled
But as the world
Still has mean
It tries to accomplish
Its own dream
It cries a tear
For everyone
Who lives in pain
Under the sun
It laughs for every
Smile we show
But when we look away
How can it know?
Have you ever wondered
What a baby dreams?
A tiny newborn baby
Of what does it dream?

Jai Hodgson (13)
Herschel Grammar School, Slough

I Had A Dream . . .

I had a dream,
That there would be an end to racism
I had a dream,
That there wouldn't be any global warming
I had a dream,
That there would be peace in this world
I had a dream,
That there would be an end to knife crime
I had a dream,
That everyone in this world could work together as one happy family
I had a dream,
That none of the animals would be hunted down
I had a dream,
That we would all love and care for each other
I had a dream,
That all little children would be able to go to school without
 any problems or hassle
I had a dream,
That everyone would have enough money to survive
I had a dream,
Those children of very young ages wouldn't have to work
 to earn their living
I had a dream,
That everyone could look forward to having a better future
I had a dream,
That there would be no hatred in this world
I had a dream,
That this dream would never end.

Sarah Ghani (13)
Herschel Grammar School, Slough

My Magical Dream

Spiders everywhere,
Fire is surrounding me.
Guns are shooting,
And blood everywhere.
That's how I dream.

Flowers and bunnies,
Cakes and trifles.
Music and laughter,
Games and dancing.
That's how I dream.

I look, no one is there,
I smell burning.
I touch the ground,
All hard and lumpy.
That's how I dream.

I look around me, lots of people,
I smell lavender and chocolate.
I touch the flowers,
How everything is so soft.
That's how I dream.

That is how I believe the world is,
Mean and dangerous,
Calm and quiet.
Rushed and hushed,
Things can never stay the same.
Everything changes.

Amrita Atwal (12)
Herschel Grammar School, Slough

I Have A Dream

I close the lips of my eyes and sleep
Hoping and longing for a pleasurable dream
Does reality have to be so real?
Are things back there what they really seem?

My life definitely has its downs
I feel the elevator won't go up
The windows of opportunity aren't so clear
And the water is only half empty in a cup

In the mornings, I don't rush to find my keys
I don't kiss my wife good day
I don't go to any job and work
But I do have to cope with what people say

How on Earth do you brush your teeth
And bathe every day of the week?
And you see a person like me
From the floor, money I seek.

Have you not guessed who I am?
I am a human being!
Just homeless in London somewhere
Let's just say I don't live like a king!

Cold winds come across my face
I wince up at the sky
My dream was a lie to my brain
So now I count the days till I die.

Joanne Hayati (13)
Herschel Grammar School, Slough

I Have A Dream

I dream of a place,
Free from disgrace,
Free from war,
Free from worries knocking at my door.
Though I want to be an RAF pilot,
I don't want to use it in a riot.
Dreams of happiness,
Not ones of pain and stress.
Bloodied streets washed clean,
More people being green.
Equal rights for everyone,
Everyone works as one.
With child labour gone,
Kids can enjoy . . . ping-pong!
Good dreams,
Bad dreams,
Horrid dreams,
Sad dreams,
Happy dreams,
Mad dreams,
Funny dreams.
Any good dream is great for me,
Sitting under the willow tree,
Lazing about carelessly,
Those are the dreams for me!

Satyam Vora (12)
Herschel Grammar School, Slough

Untitled

I dream of finding a home
But all I get is being left alone
I dream of being able to read and write
But all I get is the cold of the night
I dream of sleeping in a bed
But all I get is being left half dead
I dream of having kids and a wife
But all I get is a man with a knife
I dream of having money and wealth
But all I get is a bad impact on my health
I dream of having a phone
But all I get is a big bank loan
I dream of having something to eat
But all I get is the feeling of defeat
I dream of not being hurt
But all I get is being left in dirt
I dream of having lots of cash
But all I get is being left in trash
I dream of having a car
But all I get is being left walking under a star
I dream of being left in peace
But all I get is an argument with the police
They say dreams never do come true
But they are wrong, I say they do.

Afoo Khan (13)
Herschel Grammar School, Slough

Peace Not War

'I have a dream. I wish for a world that instead of war, there's peace,
Instead of racism, know that we are all equals.
Exclude violence, guns and knives, live in harmony, together.
Get gangs off the streets, let's all work together
And make the world a better place.'

Amy Tough (13)
Herschel Grammar School, Slough

My Dreams

Nobody knows what's going through my head
Or what I think of and dream when I'm lying in my bed
Nobody knows if I am happy or sad
Nobody knows if I've done something bad
I go to my room
I lie on my bed
I start to imagine what lies ahead
It could be exciting
It could be a bore
But at least I'm dreaming
I know that for sure
When I dream, I am all alone
I escape the world and travel to the unknown
Sometimes I see things so odd and funny
Like me jumping on a trampoline with a bunny
Nobody can ever tell who you are
Because when I'm dreaming I go so far
This just proves that when I dream
Suddenly my world seems perfect to me
Nothing's ever perfect
Nothing is always right
Not only when you dream
Is when you feel a fright.

Aneesah Mughal (12)
Herschel Grammar School, Slough

Having Dreams

I have a dream
Where I could be a superstar
Where I could shine and beam
I could play cricket
Bowling fast
And hitting the wicket
I could play football
I am short
But in a dream I am tall
But sometimes dreams are bad
A horrible one
How so very sad
I could be in a pool
And I could face a dragon
With a horrible drool
What I'm trying to say
Is dreams are unpredictable
They can be great or the other way
Sometimes my dreams are weird, most of the time
I am in a king's bed
From seven to nine
Your dreams might be black or red
Just be ready when you go to bed.

Talha Sabir (12)
Herschel Grammar School, Slough

My Dream

I have a dream of where I will be in 2016
That I hope the future will bring,
Standing on the podium, big and strong,
Until I hear the anthem song,
My family watching me with their fingers crossed,
Even my mum (she is the boss).

Back with my family,
In my humungous mansion,
Looking at my Lamborghini,
And sitting in the conservatory expansion,
My fluffy Persian cats,
Running round the house like rats.

I'm rich and wealthy,
Happy and healthy,
My own private jet,
Is my favourite pet,
My parents think, *oh my gosh!*
But I only want the dosh!

Beep! Beep! Beep!
Another gruelling 4am
Training call.

Jamie Woodman (12)
Herschel Grammar School, Slough

I Have A Nightmare

I have a nightmare that the world will never be free;
Free from the poverty that starves half the Earth's population;
Free from the cruelty that allows torture in our world's nations;
And free from the injustice that allows simply,
The outward appearance to influence the judgement of others,
In our so-called civilisations.

I have a dream that from the northernmost tip of the world
Where global warming will completely melt the vast plains of ice
Down towards Antarctica where mankind's greed
Will cause millions of defenceless animals to pay the price
From the sweltering shores of South East Asia where our pollution
Will attack the vibrant coral reefs that we cruelly sacrifice
To the west of the world where the destruction of rainforests
Will destroy our great green paradise.
Will we humans always remain engrossed in our selfish desires
To conquer over the planet's natural gems much more than suffice?

From this nightmare that haunts me to an intolerable degree,
I pray for the world to listen to my simple plea,
Please consider how your actions could give others glee,
There is only satisfaction to be derived as you will see,
For then nightmares will become blissful dreams I guarantee.

Yash Karia (15)
Herschel Grammar School, Slough

I Have A Dream . . .

I have a dream . . .
For equality between
All races and religions
All ages and genders.

I have a dream . . .
For freedom between all
Freedom of speech
Freedom or actions.

I have a dream. . .
For everyone to have a dream
However small
Or however big.

I have a dream . . .
For poverty to end
For poor to be rich
For the hungry to be full.

I have a dream . . .
For justice and fairness
With all crimes
With all issues.

Shivali Jain (10)
Herschel Grammar School, Slough

I Have A Dream

I have a dream,
No matter how silly it will seem,
I have a dream,
To better the human race.

I have a dream,
Stop war, stop pain,
Make the world a more positive place,
To better the human race.

I have a dream,
That everyone will come to their senses,
Slow down and watch out for others,
To better the human race.

I have a dream,
To block out all negatives,
Burn all bad from the world,
To better the human race.

I have a dream,
No matter how silly it will seem,
I have a dream,
To better the human race.

Robyn Campbell (12)
Herschel Grammar School, Slough

Big Dreams, Big Changes

I have a dream
To change the world
And make it a better place
For you and me.

I have a dream
To change world poverty
Help the poorer south
To be treated the same.

I have a dream
To change world racism
Stand up to all those
Who show no respect.

I have a dream
To change world judgement
Not judge people by the outside
But judge people for what they are.

I have a dream
To change the world
To make it a safer place
For every boy and girl.

Claudia Silva (12)
Herschel Grammar School, Slough

Once I Dreamed

Once I dreamed
I was a fish, swimming in the glistening sea
Once I dreamed
I was a fox, hunting for my next prey
Once I dreamed
I was a giraffe, reaching into the sky for leaves
Once I dreamed
I was a hawk, looking for food for my family to eat
Once I dreamed
I was a snake, slithering on the ground
Once I dreamed
I was a cat, frightened to have my bath
Once I dreamed
I was a monkey, jumping from branch to branch
Once I dreamed
I was a lizard, camouflaging into leaves
Once I dreamed
I was a human
Oh wait, that is reality!

Anagha Sharma (11)
Herschel Grammar School, Slough

I Have A Dream

I have a dream,
That one day I and my fellow human beings,
Will not be laughed at or joked about by
How pretty or ugly we are,
How big or small we are,
How fat or skinny we are,
How rich or poor we are,
Or by the colour of our skin.
But by the way we are with people,
And by our personalities.

Liam Addley (13)
Herschel Grammar School, Slough

Dreams

When I have a dream,
I think about what lies ahead,
My future career
And the memories I've shared!

When I have a dream,
I have these horrible thoughts,
Of me in a coffin, dead!

When I have a dream,
I have these scary feelings
Of my mum shouting, 'Get out of the house!'

When I have a dream,
I see people being cursed
And people who look scared.

At the end of my dream,
I will wake up by hearing
Beep, beep, beep from my alarm
And it is time to get dressed!

Anushka Jagpal (11)
Herschel Grammar School, Slough

Dream

Dream. I sat on a massive bird and it was flying.
Dream. It took me to an island.
Dream. The bird talked to me.
Dream. The bird said, 'My name is Magicy!'
Dream. I told him that I wanted a sports car.
Dream. A minute later there was a sports car.
Dream. I asked, 'Where am I?'
Dream. He said, 'Pink Ponk.'
Dream. I want to go back.
Dream. I am back, *cool!*
Dream. Where is my cool sports car? *Oh man!*

Jananan Krishnanandan (11)
Herschel Grammar School, Slough

My Dream

I have a dream
To have fortune and fame
The crowd screaming my name
Oh! How cool is it to be a celebrity?
Jetting of to fashion shoots
Strutting my stuff in my gorgeous black boots
Someone waiting for me, hand and foot
I'd sing my heart out to please all my fans
I'd get to the top of the charts
Doing great dancing arts
I'd be followed by paparazzi
Paparazzi taking any and every step to get in my way
But I won't care what they say
My life would be tracked 24/7
I guess being a celebrity comes with its ups and downs
It turns your feelings all around
My chances are one in a million
And I want to be that one.

Sophia Ahmad (11)
Herschel Grammar School, Slough

I Have A Dream . . .

I have a dream
With a twisting scheme
Darkness shadows the bright sky
Thick and eerie like the night's spy

The phone rings twice
I hear the squeaking of little mice
The clock strikes midnight
The end of the dream is still not in sight

Creepy sounds and creaks
Drips from the ceiling's leaks
Dangling cobwebs all around
I wish there were no sound

I can see a white light
Coming into my sight
Thump, I'm back in my bed
The next dream I'll dread.

Hannah James (13)
Herschel Grammar School, Slough

I Have A Dream . . .

My dream gave me hope,
Fantasies too.
My dream told me stories,
Made tales come true.

My dream made me act,
Not how I usually do.
My dream gave me strength,
Pulled me through.

My dream made me live,
Live right on the edge.
My dream gave me visions,
I made a pledge.

My dream made me,
Who I am today.
My dream made everything happen,
But now it slowly fades away!

Natalie Morrison (13)
Herschel Grammar School, Slough

I Have A Dream

The Earth is melting, like an ice cream in the sun,
Watching the world degrade is not my idea of fun.
The fumes of corruption sweep through the air,
None of these businessmen seem to care.

The birds fall from the sky, blackened and dark,
As the poisons of the air make their mark.
India is flooded and England is gone,
The world lies, bloody, shredded and torn.

People can't tell if it's day or night,
They sit in despair, they've lost this fight.
Plague and famine sweep through the land,
Still these people don't understand.

I have a dream,
Of a world clean and pristine,
Where pollution falls,
And God gives to all.

Sandeep Singh (12)
Herschel Grammar School, Slough

Dreams

I dream about a planet made of ice cream,
Vanilla, chocolate and strawberry.
I dream about aliens and monsters,
Anything out of the ordinary.

I dream that I'm in the future,
I dream that I'm in the past.
And then I suddenly wake up,
My dreams can never last.

Sometimes I dream I'll have loads of money,
Sometimes I dream that I won't.
Sometimes I dream about monsters,
But most of the time, I don't.

My dreams are normally wonderful,
I can do whatever I feel.
But if my dream turns into a nightmare,
I just remember, *it's not real!*

Sam Rowell (11)
Herschel Grammar School, Slough

Make Your Dream Come True

How the world is different now,
Before nobody do we bow.
The world should be a free place,
Everyone has a different face.

Mixtures of different races,
Exist happily in few places.
All people can change their ways,
To give everyone happier days.

Our world could die very soon,
Unless we stop acting like goons.
As long as there is hope, there is chance,
Along the road of happiness we could prance.

We all need to work together,
To make this world last forever.
Help us save the world,
Stop the bombs being hurled.

Sam Cheema (13)
Herschel Grammar School, Slough

Shooting Star

I really, really need a big fat star,
One that is the size of a Jaguar,
I need it to shoot like a shooting star,
So I can grant a wish that is so bizarre,
Something random, like a brand new car.

I really, really need this star,
And it looks the size of a reservoir,
I need it to fly through and past the other stars,
So I can wish away some of my hurtful scars.

I've got to get that shining star,
And now that it isn't so far,
I can guess it's huge! About the size of Mars.

And now I'm going to get my shooting star,
I can and will wish for I truly are.

Finally, I have my shooting star.

Sameer Moghal (11)
Herschel Grammar School, Slough

Nightmares And Dreams

I had a nightmare
Every night it came
And when I opened my eyes
It all stayed the same

In every war
There were soldiers dying
In every village
There were children crying

But now I have a dream
Every night it comes
People no longer fighting
Not living in the slums.

Lily Smart (13)
Herschel Grammar School, Slough

I Dream

I dream of statues standing up high
I dream of castles only up to your thigh
I dream of the world being completely changed
Or everyone being madly deranged
I dream of sitting next to the huge boiling sun
Or eating a super-sized hot dog bun
I dream, I dream, I dream

I dream of a zookeeper keeping lions tame
I dream I'm in a computer game
I dream I'm a god lying on a cloud
I dream I'm a king sitting up proud
I dream I'm a mountain stooping up high
I dream I'm as small as a common black fly
I dream I'm a giant who's really grown
I dream I'm a baby, *moan, moan, moan*
I dream, I dream, I dream.

Amar Hack (11)
Herschel Grammar School, Slough

My Perfect World

I had a dream that there was no war
Everyone was helping the poor.
Everyone was living in peace
And racism did decrease.

I had a dream that innocent animals stopped getting killed
Shelters for the homeless, the community did build
Everyone went on the bus
And no one made a fuss

I had a dream that there was no global warming
All of a sudden my perfect world was forming
Everything was serene and fine
In this perfect world of mine.

Moaiz Malik (12)
Herschel Grammar School, Slough

I Have A Dream

I have a dream
Of a war-free planet
I have a dream
Racism - I'll ban it
I have a dream
Of worldwide equality
I have a dream
To end all cruelty
I have a dream
To rid the world of child abuse
I have a dream
Of a worldwide truce
I have a dream
To put poverty in the past
I have a dream
To make the world last!

Asad Ahmed (12)
Herschel Grammar School, Slough

I Have A Dream

I have a dream that all wars will stop
and peace will come forever
and all will be treated the same whatever their colour
Or their personality and religion.

I have a dream that poverty will come to an end
and all will become equal
especially the poor countries with poor facilities
that will, for once, become wealthy.

I have a dream that the Credit Crunch will come to an end
and everyone will get their jobs back.

I have a dream that global warming will come to an end
and the whole world and both Poles will not melt
and we can keep the extraordinary animals so that we can show
each of our generation how amazing these animals actually are.

Tarnjot Virdee (11)
Herschel Grammar School, Slough

Perfect World

I have a dream that everyone gets along
And no one does anything wrong.

I have a dream of a world with no pain
And there won't be abuse towards the insane.

I have a dream for solar-powered cars
And no one gets into smoking cigars.

I have a dream that no one gets assassinated
And everyone is exhilarated.

I have a dream of a safe chatroom
And no threats of terror or doom.

I have a dream that the world will live in peace
And there won't be any need for the police.

Aditya Arjun (12)
Herschel Grammar School, Slough

Season For Change

First blossom in spring
What happened to it?
First golden leaf in autumn
Where did it go?
If only we noticed these things
All things bright and beautiful
Animals and creatures too
But time ticks away
Life rushes past
Nothing stays long enough
For you to realise it's there.
Seasons come and go
People come and go
I have a dream
That time will stop.

Manveet Dhaliwal (13)
Herschel Grammar School, Slough

You And I Are The Future

I decided long ago that the pen was mightier than the sword.
Fights and violence have never got us anywhere
and they never will.
It may only need one solitary voice to make a difference.
A single word to change a future, to make things happen.
In my dreams the words to make things happen will be spoken,
someone with the courage will speak up.
Our fates, our futures, the livelihood of the Earth lie in our hands.
Each and everyone matters and can make a difference
whether our skin is black, brown or white.
You can speak those words of difference and make the world
a better place.
You matter, you can make a difference.
You, like me, are the future.

Kate Horwell (12)
Herschel Grammar School, Slough

My Dream Poem

My dream is to be in an army fighting a war,
My dream is to be a rich man that helps the poor,
My dream is to stand on the stars,
My dream is to be in the Grand Prix racing fast cars,
My dream is to make a game,
My dream is to have a lot of fame,
My dream is to write a book,
My dream is to cure people that cannot look,
My dream is to be able to fly,
My dream is to be able to jump to the sky,
My dream is to have a bit company,
My dream is to make lots of money,
I hope my dreams come true
Or I will feel blue.

Hassam Kashmiri
Herschel Grammar School, Slough

United

I have a dream
That one day
There will be a big fire,
So massive that it will consume the fuel like a hungry beast
And the fuel will be anger
And racism
And all hatred,
So all that will be left burning are the embers
Of what was an inferno of divide.
Dust to dust, ashes to ashes and Earth to Earth.
Black to white.
Rich to poor and so all the divides in this world will be gone
And we will all be
United together.

Jack Porter (12)
Herschel Grammar School, Slough

If Only - (I Have A Dream)

If only
The world had no fear or hate
If only
People would stop ruining what God did create
If only
Knife crime did no longer exist
If only
Different cultures were not simply dismissed
If only
Children were not abused
If only
Women were unbruised
If only
People were not controlled by drugs
If only
We were not in fear of thugs
If only
Terrorists did not petrify us
If only
There weren't diseases that were cureless
If only
There was no pain
If only
There were no sick games
If only
There was no poverty
If only
We were not scared of what lurks in a dark alley.

Only if
People would stop to think
Throw away the drugs and drink
Only if
People would lend a helping hand
To everyone from the polar ice caps to the desert land
Only if
We put an end to this right now
We do not let it, we do not allow.

Jodie Reilly (13)
Hertswood Lower School, Borehamwood

Today, Tomorrow

Today
A distorted world
Testing times and distressing news
A rough and jumbled life for everyone
A fame-addicted nation with troublemakers and trouble takers
A guilt-stricken world for the permanent stain it's left
                                              on its environment
Poverty and riches galore
Starvation and indulgence
Neglect and popularity
Selflessness and greed
People dying and not a second thought
An unfair world

Tomorrow
Needs change
It needs its people with riches to share
Starvation to be stopped
Greed to be put behind
For us to care about each other

And I have a dream
That little by little
And step by step
We can get to tomorrow
Together.

Simeon Nichols (14)
Hertswood Lower School, Borehamwood

I Have A Dream

I have a dream that one day I can stop for a moment,
To make people realise that what we are doing is destroying London town,
Killing for the most petty reasons,
Getting involved in gangs,
Killing each other for pride, for dignity,
Losing a life is not worth it,
It causes pain, grief and sometimes guilt.

Knives, guns, anything to get rid of a life,
Does it ever occur that this is a crime to people?
The victim hasn't even lived their life,
One shot, one sound and a life is dead and gone,
Some suffer in silence,
Knowing that their life will pass before their eyes tomorrow.

Enjoy life, do well,
Why should you waste your time in prison?
Make something of yourself,
Be inspirational to the next generation.

If we stand together,
Let's tell a young person that carrying a knife or a gun is bad,
As one we should fight against this terror,
This pain, this hurt is not worth it,
Let's speak and tell that what youths are doing is wrong.

Ratidzo Masunda (13)
Hertswood Lower School, Borehamwood

Never Forgotten

(In memory of my uncle Norman, 05/07/47-04/03/09)

The heavens opened and fell out of the sky
A great man of wisdom and love,
Nothing to his name, not even a cry.

A lily starts at the bottom and rises to the top.
Happy and sad times occur.
Every star has to drop.
Breaking religion's powerful chains
Following his family's hatred
But the drug of love has no pain.
His clever, intelligence power
His love, care is tall
His fruits, lemons are not sour.
You may not be here to comfort me through bad.
I was unaware how strong my love was for you.
You, as a wonderful man, would tell me not to be sad.
He will always be in my heart and soul.
The memory of his smiling face.
The li'l birdy on my shoulder.
Every runner comes to a bend.
Every miracle has an end.
However you,
You will not be forgotten.

Molly McDonagh (14)
Hertswood Lower School, Borehamwood

No!

Let's say *no!*
Let's say *no* to bullying
Say *no* to war
Say *no* to terrorists
Say *no* to anything that gets in our way
Let's stand up and say *no!*

What's stopping us saying *no?*
A bully may punch us
A bully may verbally abuse us
But a bully will not stop us from saying *no!*

What's stopping us saying *no?*
A war may split our world apart
A war can kill the most innocent of people
But a war will not stop us from saying *no!*

What's stopping us saying *no?*
A terrorist may destroy lives.
A terrorist may never end until ultimate carnage is achieved
But a terrorist will not stop us from saying *no!*

What's stopping us saying *no?*
There should be nothing that stops us
We should be able to stand up and say *no!*
Nothing should stop us from saying that word, *no!*

Ben Molyneux (14)
Hertswood Lower School, Borehamwood

Family

F amilies are the best
A nd sometimes they can be a pest
M y mum is the best and wears a beautiful dress
I' ll always remember my family helping me out
L ittle times I run about
Y eah, that's me and that's my family.

Chloe Hayes (11)
Hertswood Lower School, Borehamwood

My Chocolate Land

Here I am in Chocolate Land
With flowers in my hand.
Walking down the chocolate sand
With my girlfriend, hand in hand.

My girlfriend thinks I'm funny
As cute as a chocolate bunny.
She loves it when it's sunny
And she likes a bit of honey.

We're on our way to the shop
We are buying some pop.
She wears a chocolate top
And her daddy is a cop.

We are walking across the beach
I'm about to make a speech.
Then she's about to reach
For her chocolate bleach.

Here I am in Chocolate Land
With nothing in my hand.
Walking across the chocolate sand
With no girlfriend hand in hand.

Callan Jones (11)
Hertswood Lower School, Borehamwood

Senses

I have no hearing, sense of touch, smell or vision
nothing, so I'll just have to use my precision
I'll just have to stay where I am
and be as quiet as a baby lamb
but slowly, slowly, as in a flutter
back they come, now life is better.
It's as if now I am more free
more free from harsh reality.

Jack McMaster (12)
Hertswood Lower School, Borehamwood

My Inspiration (I Have A Dream)

There is always one person that makes a drastic change to the world
one person that inspires us to be better, dream bigger
and strive for perfection.
This could be anyone, anywhere.

One gesture could change a life.
someone's style or the way they react to certain situations
could be a guide to others.
Someone's success could teach others to work harder;
someone's failure could also be an inspiration to better ourselves.

One person's life could be an inspiration to the world.
Inspiration varies from one to the next;
different things inspire different people.
Something that may be considered as irrelevant could mould
the minds of millions.

Some people dedicate their lives to inspire,
for some it's as natural as breathing.
But one must always try to be an inspiration to others
in any way possible,
because by doing so one person can affect the world.

Annique Debeauville (14)
Hertswood Lower School, Borehamwood

You Will Be Remembered

M y family, I love.
Y ou are my friend.

F amous you can be
A nd you're never wrong.
M y friends will always be remembered.
 I like everyone to always be the same.
L ike me, I like you.
Y ou're my friend.

Jordan Saville (11)
Hertswood Lower School, Borehamwood

My Mates!

My mates, well how can I put this . . . ?
Our friendship isn't seen with our eyes, it's felt within our hearts,
We are together for the good times and we make it through the bad,
You can tell me and I can tell you,
We make no judgements in what we say,
I'm here for you all every single day.

I know we can argue and say some hurtful things,
But when I see you crying, my heart is torn apart,
And I hope you know I will wipe your eyes
And mend your broken heart,
And can't wait to see what the future brings.

Just remember this is who I am and that is who you are,
Don't ever change or we will break apart.

Also, Stephanie, she is my best friend and I hope I can be that back,
I know we argue an awful lot but I'm proud of the friends we are
And the friendship we've got!

Remember I love you!

Chloe Livermore (12)
Hertswood Lower School, Borehamwood

Great Ormond Street Hospital

'Just one more time, hold on tight love,
last injection and it will stop.'
Since I was a baby, now into a teen,
I've been going to Great Ormond Street.
It's filled with laughter, fun and joy,
clowns with red noses helping little kids
through a hard day.
As the doctor says, 'Just go to sleep
and it will be better in the morning.'
I know it won't be.
I just want to be like everyone else.

Connie O'Connell (12)
Hertswood Lower School, Borehamwood

My Friends Are My Heroes

My friends I love, I hold them so near,
My friends I love, I hold them so dear,
My days were blank, my life a bore,
Colourless and senseless is my life no more.
They made me see the world's big light,
Now to lose them, I won't go down without a fight.
Thanks to them my life is just right.

My friends I love, they're the best you can get,
My friends I love, I'm so glad that we met,
They give me a drive to see tomorrow,
They help me through to cure all my sorrows.
They put the colour in my eye, they are the reason I feel great,
Now I can't live my life without such a good mate.

I don't need a perfect sister, I don't need a perfect end,
I don't need the newest phone, not even the latest trend,
I don't need Pandora's hope, not even for a day,
I just need my not-so-perfect friends, to help me through the day.

Shannon Kane (12)
Hertswood Lower School, Borehamwood

A Bad Habit

You think it's cool, you think it's fun
but when you're sixty, you'll be done
The habit attacks like a wild animal
you think you're crazy, you think you're mad
but to everyone else you're just sad
It will take over you like a plug in the brain
and when you're seventy, you'll be insane

So quit!

Act while the heart is young
don't just leave it
and get cancer on the tongue!

Adrian Bernstein (12)
Hertswood Lower School, Borehamwood

I Have A Dream

The first black president
His name is Barack Obama
He came from Philadelphia
Now he's a bit wealthier

He now lives in the White House
Now Bush is gone
His speeches to the nation
Cause fantastic sensations

The thoughts of his mind
Have inspired many people
He's one of a kind
He's Barack Obama

Barack Obama inspires me
He's a great man
Like he says,
'Yes we can!'

Emmanuel Banjo (14)
Hertswood Lower School, Borehamwood

What Can I Be?

They spoke up in the silence,
They stood up when everyone was lying down,
They looked up when others looked away,
They smiled through the rivers of tears,
They found a trail when others got lost,
They held their dreams high so they wouldn't get crushed,
They aimed for the stars and got the moon,
They stood up for what they believed,
They made a difference,
They inspired me.

This is what I can be.

Cara Elvins
Hertswood Lower School, Borehamwood

I Have A Dream To Change The World!

I have a dream to change the world,
preventing people smoking,
it causes cancer and bad lungs,
which leads to suffering.

I have a dream to change the world,
preventing wars,
people losing their houses and relatives,
which makes them very poor.

I have a dream to change the world,
stop bullying occurring,
everybody gets more friendly
making them mature.

I have a dream to change the world,
hope everything I said becomes true,
it will make the world better,
and make it a better place for *you!*

Tae Kyung Baek (12)
Hertswood Lower School, Borehamwood

My Mum

My mum I love, I tell her everything,
She's caring and funny,
I love her so much,
She's always there for me,
When I'm down and in a grump.

My mum I love, she's brought me up,
The hurtful things I say that make her cry,

I'm here now to wipe your eyes.
I value you a lot and would hate to lose you,
I am so glad that you're my mum.

Samantha Lewis (12)
Hertswood Lower School, Borehamwood

I Have A Dream

I have a dream to change the world
For people who are less fortunate than us
Like people with cancer, meningitis and pneumonia.

They cannot do as much as us
Because they are seriously ill
And some of them are very young
Aged five months to one hundred years old.

They are on the road to dying
Because of these serious conditions
If people could raise a little money for them
It would change their lives.

They would be able to play with friends
Who they hadn't seen in months
It would be like starting their life again
And they could do all the things they'd like to do.

Louise Munting (12)
Hertswood Lower School, Borehamwood

The NBL Poem!

You have been a friend, you have been a foe.
Why you waste your time, I'll never know.
But you were there, through thick and thin,
Only waiting to be let in.
You have been the one to inspire me to live.
You showed me how to laugh, joke and to forgive.
Only you have been able to see inside
Those feelings I've tried to hide.
You will always be an amazing part of me.
You showed me how to be the best that I can be.
You're always there to listen, you trust me in return,
Because of you, I will live on
My only hope is that you stay as strong.

Lucy Starnes, Nicole Antonio & Billie Hampson (13)
Hertswood Lower School, Borehamwood

The Biggest Dream

I dream that there will be no war in the world, that everyone
will live in peace.
But I also have a dream that we will all believe in ourselves
as much as our teacher, parent and friend believe in us,
I must add why . . .
If you can't believe in yourself, what makes you think other people
will believe in you?

Also, if you don't believe in yourself, you may not achieve what
you really can.

I dream of many things but not all things come true
but if you give it your best you are achieving something
and that is none other than your dream.
You may not be the best at it but you are who you are.

And that is my dream:
to identify yourself but also become that person.

Mink Goodman (14)
Hertswood Lower School, Borehamwood

One Day

One day bullies will be no more
One day someone will close that door
One day children will be full of glee
The person who closes that door will be me

One day bullies will be gone forever
One day bullies will become clever
One day 'bully' will be a word of past tense
Bullies will come to their senses

One day we will stamp them out
One day we will wipe out this spout
One day bullies will be terminated
They will be exterminated.

Jack McWilliam (14)
Hertswood Lower School, Borehamwood

My Mum

My mother's name is Marlene,
she's always there for me,
she's been there for my birthdays, my celebrations too,
she's been my light through my life,
even through the tough times,
she's been there for my brother,
and works so hard too.
She wipes my tears and hugs me tight,
tells me everything will be alright.
She makes me feel so happy even when I'm sad,
she buys me clothes and gives me a home,
and makes sure that I'm warm.
This is who my hero is
for now and evermore.

Chase Rochester (12)
Hertswood Lower School, Borehamwood

The Shadow

There was a party at night,
I got bored,
so I decided to leave,
it was really dark so I started to panic,
I could see someone following me,
I started to run, he was running too,
I faced my fear,
and turned around and noticed
that no one was there,
I carried on walking,
he was walking too,
and I looked around one last time,
and saw that it was my shadow,
I was running from me!

Tom McConnon-Evans & Scott Lindsey (13)
Hertswood Lower School, Borehamwood

I Have A Dream

My dream is -
I want to stand up to a bully
I want bullying to stop
bullying makes people sad
bullying is very bad
I look up to Fabregas
Fabregas is the best
he can take the test
I want a million pounds
I need to win one grand
and want to see my sister in a band
I need to win the grand prize
then my family won't be so poor
I want to walk through my front door to fame!

Sam Prangnell (12)
Hertswood Lower School, Borehamwood

Sisterly Love

They always make me smile.
They always make me laugh.
They are precious to me like a gem,
That does not want to be lost.
They take me shopping, then to the park.
If I am upset they are there for me.
They mean the world to me.
I speak to them on the phone,
And the bills are loads!
But I don't care.
They are my sisters and I love them
When they are sick I hug and kiss them.
I don't care if I catch their cold.
They are the best sisters in the world.

Annabelle Lisowski (11)
Hertswood Lower School, Borehamwood

Untitled

What is life to me?
Happiness, the right to be free?
None of the above is correct
So sit back and reflect.

As I am here, free as a bird
To me it occurred
That whilst I am happy, joyful and alive
I know some may not survive.

Whilst children live in poverty, war zones and mud huts
Ill, hurt or dying
As wars breaks out, as people die, I shall not lie
I feel the urge to cry.

Charlie Bowsher (12)
Hertswood Lower School, Borehamwood

I Have A Dream - Football

The skills they show inspire me,
The crowds shouting their names,
The lights of the stadium raining down upon them,
I hope one day that could be me.

The money,
The fame,
That lifestyle,
I hope one day that that can be me.

I need this,
I want this,
It's all I've ever wanted, the skills, the money, the fame,
Will I ever get it? It will all be mine . . . one day

Frank Harrison (14)
Hertswood Lower School, Borehamwood

Stop Drugs

Drugs are bad,
they make you go mad,
Don't get addicted
or you'll become afflicted.

They make you ill,
and mess up your life.
They stain your fingers
and get in your brain.

They make you sad
and you will not be glad.
Do you want to die
just so you can get high?

Shannon Hurley (12)
Hertswood Lower School, Borehamwood

Imagine

Could you imagine
Meeting the one who inspired you?
Could you imagine
Inspiring someone else?
Could you imagine
Reaching your greatest goals?
Could you imagine
Being as big as Cheryl Cole
Or even Madonna?
Could you imagine
A perfect world?

Just imagine!

Jade Anne Perry (12)
Hertswood Lower School, Borehamwood

No More Drugs

Drugs are stupid,
Drugs are bad,
When I see them,
I go mad.
If you take them,
Then that's OK,
But when you get arrested
For being thugs,
Don't look at me,
Say 'No!' to drugs.

Chris Gee (11)
Hertswood Lower School, Borehamwood

Inspire

Tom Sykes inspires me
He wins a race.
He is proud of winning.

My dad inspires me.
I love my dad.
My dad loves me.

But that's all who inspire me.

Paige McClintock (11)
Hertswood Lower School, Borehamwood

Who Inspires Me?

My mum inspires me.
She sits on her bed in the morning, putting her make-up on.
When you are upset she makes you smile.
My mum inspires me.
She is the best.
Sometimes I think to myself how lucky I am.
I love my mummy, she is the best!

Ellen Carrick (12)
Hertswood Lower School, Borehamwood

Beckham

B all skills
E nthusiastic
C ool dude
K icking
H ard tackles
A mazing
M agnificent.

Ben Larter (11)
Hertswood Lower School, Borehamwood

I Had A Dream . . .

A dream of being a princess,
A dream of climbing trees.

A dream of saving animals,
A dream of sailing the sea.

But most importantly . . .
A dream of being *me*.

Chelsea Pritchard (12)
Hertswood Lower School, Borehamwood

I Have A Dream!

I have a dream that one day I can fly.
I have a dream that one day I can touch the sky.
I have a dream that I can be a footballer.
I have a dream I can be much taller.
I have a dream that I can always eat ice cream.
I have a dream everything I do will be extreme!

Jake Blyth (11)
Hertswood Lower School, Borehamwood

I Have A Dream

Racism affects everyone in one way or another,
'Why do we have to be different?' a child may ask his mother.
It's not just physical, but psychological too,
People are racist because they only think their kind is true.

People see us differently just because of the colour of our skin,
People treat us differently, even though we are the same within.
People speak to us differently, because we look different from them,
But we are really the same, as all those white women, children and men.

People see us differently because of our beliefs,
Mainly at Christmas when, upon our door, there is no wreath.
Just because we live in a Christian country, doesn't mean we must be too,
We all should be able to live as neighbours, no matter
                        what religion we belong to.

We must tackle racism together,
Alone, we will make no more difference than a feather!
At one point in their life, everyone will experience this,
But don't let it get to you, now listen to my wish.

I have a dream that one day we will all live alongside,
Where colour and religion do not matter, only what is on the inside.

Jade Clapich (14)
JFS School, Kenton

I Have A Dream

I have a dream,
Of a world,
Where no one judges,
And no one keeps grudges,
Where people look each other in the eye,
And when one person looks at another,
They see not their face,
Or religion or race,
They see within,
Because we are all equal.

I have a dream,
Of a world,
Where people comfort the sensitive,
And support the weak,
Encourage the inexperienced,
And respect the knowledgeable,
Where people strive to be like the one,
Who isn't the most famous or beautiful,
But the kindest, and the one who knows best.

I have a dream,
Of a world,
Where being rude is still frowned upon,
And not expected,
Where rape is still shocking,
And not part of everyday news,
Where murder is still heartbreaking,
And not a passing thought,
Where the horrors of the streets,
Are still rare,
And leave a shiver down your spine.

I have a dream,
Of a world,
When people leave their seats,
To give those unable to stand,
Because they want to,
Not because they must,
Where when a person goes to the doctor's,

They get treated with kindness, not impatience,
And are counted as an individual,
And not as one of many.

I have a dream,
Of a world,
Where people smile for nothing,
Just because maybe,
They might brighten someone's day,
Where when a person falls to the ground,
Someone is right there to help them up again,
Regardless of who they are.

These dreams,
Different colours and shapes and sizes,
Some flickering and some bold,
Some connected with each other,
Some on opposite sides,
Some like dominoes,
Others free-standing,
All different, but all important.

That the world be united,
That people are kind,
And supportive of one another,
Where people respect nature,
And each other,
No more fights, no more war,
The list is endless, is it not?

But what I want,
What my dream *really* is,
Is that people do everything they can,
To make this world,
As good as it can get.

Elinor Roth (14)
JFS School, Kenton

I Have A Dream

When I was young
Just a little white girl
I was different from others
I had a dream

When I saw a muddy puddle
I would not jump
I would smile and stare
And dream of a world

A world in the walls
Of the safe brown clouds
It was secret and safe
It was a dream

There was colour and sun
There were smiles and laughs
There were hopes and wishes
There in my dream

There were black people
There were white people
There were all kinds of people
There in my dream

But the rain dried up
The muddy puddle was gone
So were the smiles
It was just a dream

In the real world, things had changed
I had woken up
My dreams were coming true

Our world, this world, will be ours forever
Our skin, this skin, will be ours forever
Our family, this family, will be ours forever
Our dreams, this dream, will be ours forever.

Ella Landsman (14)
JFS School, Kenton

I Have A Dream!

I have a dream that there will be no pollution
Trees, plants, animals will live
Everyone will do something to help
Recycle, electricity and walk, they will give

I have a dream, do not hurt or kill
Everyone like friends and family
No fights or arguments, *never!*
If everyone does something, we will be there,
Nearly

I have a dream there are no more fears
A dream of just happiness
Everything that happens is good
Tears and crying will be less

I have a dream, good and bad
Some dreams are not for you to hear
However, some are bright and jolly
Prices go cheap not dear

I have a dream that everyone will believe in themselves
People will be accepted the same
No one will be made fun of
One another called a good name

I have a dream, a dream that's completely you
A dream of you, a dream of me
Your dream, our dream
Something for you to do

I have a dream that black and white are equal
In fact, all religions never treated differently
People in the world hand in hand
I have a dream no one's different.

Chloe Rich (14)
JFS School, Kenton

I Believe

I believe that the Messiah will come,
And rescue us from our slovenly slum,

When people ask me what I want from life,
I answer, happiness, kids and a wonderful wife,

My dreams are simple and the meaning is clear,
That one day I will find, what to me is so dear,

I dream of us all living a life that is happy,
No longer sadness, let's make it snappy,

I take for granted what I get for being good,
When others are thankful for scraps of food,

I sit and wonder and believe in my mind,
That together we can build one mankind,

Not Arabs, Christians, Muslims or Jews,
But as one, together, what've we got to lose?

Then the people ask me, 'How will you do it?'
So I reply, 'Not by myself but as a single unit.'

Working together for a better world,
With love, kindness, it can all be unfurled,

I want my children to have a wonderful life,
Not one that is full of horrors and awful strife,

Together, if we do it, my dreams will be finished,
No longer will children's dreams be diminished,

One day I'm sure my dreams will come true,
And together we will fix this, me and you.

Matt Polden (14)
JFS School, Kenton

I Have A Dream
Words To Change The World . . .

I have a dream
That there is peace.
That everyone will get along,
And all the troubles will decease.

I have a dream,
That there will be no such thing as slave labour,
That everybody will be treated equally,
And we will live side by side, just like neighbours.

I have a dream,
That people in Africa will see a lifetime ahead of them.
That they will live in comfort and sleep in beds,
And in the end, all the starving children will be fed.

I have a dream,
That people will recognise,
That sometimes you have to see,
Things through other people's eyes.

I have a dream,
That everybody will play fair,
That no one will be selfish,
And that fighting and cursing, nobody will even dare.

I have a dream,
That everyone else will have the same dream as me,
That this is not just a school poem that teaches you mortality,
But might just possibly, become reality.

Nivi Kanel (13)
JFS School, Kenton

I Had A Dream

Many, many years ago
There was a time that no one would want to go back to
A time that no one, whether they were black or white,
Would want to return to that struggle and fight

A fight that would make your blood boil
For what the black nation had to toil
It wasn't going to get any better, or that's what it seemed
Apart from one man, a man who had a dream

A dream that was extremely dangerous to share
But he shared it anyway, for his nation he cared
So in that inspiring year of 1963
He made a speech in hope they would be free

But his dream was like playing with fire
Very dangerous and the consequences were dire
But he went through with it no matter what people said
It was in the year 1968 his body lay dead

Today we all stand here as one together
Hard to forget those hard times forever
We will always remember this one man
Who fought on his own but was never alone
The man who quoted: *'I am happy to join with you today*
In what will go down in history as the greatest demonstration
For freedom in the history of our nation'.

Martin Luther King.

Georgia Lubert (14)
JFS School, Kenton

I Had A Dream

Last night I dreamt a funny dream
Of sitting on a hill.
It was late at night and I was
Getting quite a chill.

Confronted by a black man
Who offered me his coat.
Such a shame that that man
Never had the right to vote.

He told me of his troubles
And how he dreamed of being free
To walk the Earth with no fear
Of the likes of you and me.

Though I would never hurt him
I know that others might
For being slightly different
But that's no excuse to fight.

They don't see the bigger picture
Of the friendly man inside,
They judge him by his skin
Which just denies him of his pride.

For that man is our equal
Just the same as me and you.
And as I sat upon that hill
I prayed his dream would soon come true.

Sebastian Tuckman (14)
JFS School, Kenton

I Had A Dream

I had a dream,
    no jokes about Jews,
    no massacres of Muslims,
    no beatings of black people.

I had a dream,
    no wars between nations,
    no stabbings,
    no bombs.

I had a dream,
    no need for an army,
    no need for a navy,
    no need for defence at all.

I had a dream,
    no crack,
    no weed,
    no drugs in existence.

I had a dream,
    no drunks,
    no smokers,
    no druggies too.

I had a dream . . .
    then I woke up.

Boaz Goldwater (14)
JFS School, Kenton

I Have A Dream

I have a dream where all people are equal,
Where a man is not judged by appearance,
Where a man is not judged at all,
Because if we are all equal, how can we judge each other?

It is easier to find problems in others,
But harder to find the problems in yourself.
If you were to judge a man,
Do it by his character.

People do not choose their skin colour,
But we should be proud of it anyway.
I have a dream that some day my kids won't have to deal with racism,
And will be free people and not discriminated against.

I have a dream that some day I can ride in the front of a bus,
And pay the fair price at a shop.
I have a dream to be served at any restaurant without trouble,
America is a great nation filled with opportunity,
But it isn't good enough.

I have a dream for the world to be a better place,
Where I have all the same rights as any man.
I have a dream for our people to be treated fairly,
I have a dream.

Elie Kraft (13)
JFS School, Kenton

I Have A Dream . . .

There is a world today, there was a world yesterday, and a world
for tomorrow.
We dream of the future because we have lived in the past.
Sorrow, happiness, they are just directions, pulling us to our own destinies.
But what do we get?
We have lived in worlds of racism.
One man had a dream that those worlds would disappear,
and be replaced by worlds of love and care.
Do we live in that world?
Now I have a dream,
I have a dream that love and care will go everywhere.
Now we may have it here,
Some might have it elsewhere,
But it is not everywhere.
I have a dream that we are not strong, smart, charming,
in ways of hate.
Can't we have that in love? In freedom?
Why can't the world stop hiding their minds in shadow,
And speak out, and learn what you really want in life?
I have a dream that Man can become what Man thinks.
No disguises, no cloaks, red, blue, green . . .
Just Man.

Dan Hadary (13)
JFS School, Kenton

Utopia

I have a dream
A song to sing
To help us through reality

I have the dream of equality
All races, religions and cultures to come together as one

I have the vivid dream of world peace
For neighbours to listen to one another
Stop the fighting
Stop the starvation
Stop the killings

If we all come together
If we all help each other
The outside should not matter
It's what's inside that counts

A person's personality means so much more
So please stand by me and follow what I saw

Deep in the forest the peaceful bird she sings
For the hope of what tomorrow will bring
Does anybody listen?

Georgia Bass (13)
JFS School, Kenton

I Have A Dream

I have a dream,
That all people in this world of fear,
Will come together, causing no more tears,
Peace will come and save us all,
Keeping us standing, brave and tall.

I have a dream,
That peace will stop this war,
Of love and hate, religion and more,
We are all one world,
A community, living together,
We should not be suffering from things like war,
We should only be suffering from things like bad weather.

I have one more dream, much like the others,
We are all the same, all from our mothers,
All that separates us is the colour of our skin,
Or social group we are in,
So let's stop all of this and put it to one side,
Just think for a second and you may realise.

I have a dream that one day may be a reality.

Daniel Sugarman (14)
JFS School, Kenton

I Have A Dream

I have a dream . . .

I have a dream that there will be no wars for oil in the Middle East,
I have a dream that the world will conserve energy,
I have a dream that scientists will find another source of energy,
I have a dream that people will stop destroying the Earth,

I have a dream . . .

I have a dream that people will stop cutting down the rainforest,
I have a dream that people stop littering the streets,
I have a dream that pollution in major cities is lowered,
I have a dream that the drugs trade is brought to a halt,

I have a dream . . .

I have a dream that racism is stopped,
I have a dream that every company has Fairtrade,
I have a dream that more money is given to the NHS,
I have a dream that no one uses children as soldiers.

I have a dream that will last a lifetime!

Charles Langsford (14)
JFS School, Kenton

I Have A Dream

A dream is a wish your heart makes
When you feel really passionate about something
A dream is a friend
When those around you have left you in the dark with nothing
A dream is a belief
When others are doing wrong
Don't stand back and not do anything
A dream is a hope
When you pray for the best
With hope you'll fulfil everything
A dream is a wish your heart makes . . .

Gabrielle Abadi (14)
JFS School, Kenton

Reach For The Stars

I have a dream
And I know it might be a little extreme
But I will not stop
Until I get to the top

I know I won't stop till
I get every single thrill
I want to go to space
And maybe visit the base

Everyone says how hard it is
I might have to be a rocket whizz
But I will always try my best
To be better than the rest

So next time you look up
You might see me shooting up
And achieving everything I ever wanted.

Yuval Cohen (13) & Soheil Assil (14)
JFS School, Kenton

I Have A Dream

When I grow up, I may be tall,
Professionally playing basketball.
But what do I know? I'm only fourteen,
A grumpy teenager, spotty and mean.

A journalist, doctor or an author,
I find all of these a bit of a bore.
Maybe a painter or a designer,
I will make chairs, perhaps recliners.

Now it's the end, what have I learnt?
All of your dreams get shattered and burnt!

Adam Childs (13)
JFS School, Kenton

Freedom

Freedom, is the word only to be dreamt of?
Is the word freedom only to be whispered on the lips
of suffering slaves?
Dreamt fleetingly by those yearning for justice?
That single word that gave hope to so many souls in the midst
of hardship.
People who used to work all day and get nothing back in return.
Through their clouds of oppression, glimpses of sunlight did appear.
They lent courage to those who had long forgotten the promise
of freedom.
The sun has not yet fully risen over the clouds of despair.
But we can only hope that equality will pierce the minds of others,
as the sun still rises.
No matter what colour or creed they are, there will always be hope
to guide others in darkness.

Laura Imzayin (14)
JFS School, Kenton

Dreams On Flying

I have a dream to be:

A pilot in the sky,
Floating very high
Above deep blue seas,
Zooming past down beneath,
Seeing diamond ripples below as we fly.

The warm patchwork of fields,
As the quilt of the English countryside
The cotton wool clouds,
Like a perfect painting
The pilot. The only person to see it.
That is, unless you want to have a ride.
Flight! That unique science!
One thing: any passengers? You'll need some reliance!

Elliott Scott (14)
JFS School, Kenton

I Have A Dream

I have a dream there'll be no more men like him
Men that play and smell so grim
I have a dream with no wars, no fights,
No brothers that kick, no brothers that bite
I have a dream where there are no schools
With their horrid food and their freezing pools
I have a dream for a world of peace
With no men that smell so grim, no war and brothers
That fight, no horrid schools with horrid food
That's what I dream, but it's only a dream.

Katie Dawson (13)
Kingham Hill School, Chipping Norton

My Dream

I have a dream,
about a world with no wars,
with not one innocent's scream.

Where life is not lost,
in just a heartbeat,
at such an unforgivable cost.

Where blood isn't drawn,
on once happy times,
and everyone isn't dead at dawn.

Where the green, lush fields,
can grow and grow,
and not be trampled by boot heels.

Where children can laugh and play
with their fathers,
and everyone can be happy and gay.

Please don't let them scream,
put in the effort,
and let this not just be a dream.

Alice Hilborn (13)
Kingham Hill School, Chipping Norton

Life

I have a dream to live a second life
Or to live forever with someone I love
My life goes quickly like a cloud in the sky
Once there, then gone forever.

I have a dream to live my life right
To make sure I do it properly
Not to waste my life away
Like the food I eat.

I have a dream to be a great mum
Loving and caring for my children
Always there for them
I'd never leave them.

I have a dream to die after a happy life
To be grateful for the life I have been given
To love the world as I once did
And to share the word of God.

Sophie Laing (12)
Kingham Hill School, Chipping Norton

I Dreamed A Dream Of Heaven

I dreamed that she'd be there
Beside me once again
To go to the woods and watch the deer
And rabbits bound around.

To run barefoot in the grass
On a hot summer's day
To feel the sunbeams whilst sitting on the hay.

She has gone to the most beautiful place
Called Heaven
But she will always be in my heart.

Where she has gone
She deserves all the love she will get
The one I love
My little girl

My baby Corset.

Leya Womersley (13)
Kingham Hill School, Chipping Norton

I Have A Dream!

I have a dream that I will not be forgotten.
I have a dream that I will be remembered.
I have a dream that I will be loved.
I have a dream that I will go to Heaven.
I have a dream that I will help others.
I have a dream that I will be respected.
I have a dream that I have earned the right to live on Earth.

Now I am here alone, and defenceless.
I don't like this place, where am I?
I run and I run.
I am just going around in circles.
I stop and sit down and curl up in a ball.
I see dark figures circling around me.
Where am I? What happened?
I don't like this place.
I'm all alone!

Joshua Goddard (13)
Kingham Hill School, Chipping Norton

I Believe

I believe that equal rights,
Will bring an end to all the fights,
Our hopes are flying,
To all; do not stop trying.

I believe that stopping wars,
Will stop people from breaking laws,
People need to stop lying,
To all; do not stop trying.

I believe that more peace,
Will get racism to cease,
From harmony, people need to stop shying,
To all; do not stop trying.

Simon Dyer (13)
Margaret Beaufort Middle School, Riseley

I Have A Dream

In my world,
A world of freedom
A land of peace,
Sorrow and racism are gone,
People are created equally.

In our kingdom,
A world of freedom
A land of peace,
Let freedom reign,
Let brotherhood reign.

In our land,
A world of freedom
A land of peace,
Every hill and mountain shall be made low,
The rough places shall be made plain
And the crooked places shall be made straight.

Within our walls,
A world of freedom
A land of peace,
White and black children,
Catholics and Protestants,
Jews and Gentiles
Will hold hands, and sing together.

In our country,
A world of freedom
A land of peace,
Free at last; free at last.
The sweltering heat of oppression
Shall stop!

Alastair Declan Sparham (13)
Margaret Beaufort Middle School, Riseley

I Wanna Be . . .

Pole position
Watch the lights . . .
It's *go!*
Bogging start
Burning rubber
Squealing tyres
Bursting tyres
Disastrous first corner
McLaren handling
Ferrari speed
Goodbye Honda
Hello BrawnGP
Boiling sun
Soaking wet
Turbo chargers
Big V8s
Engine blow-up
Flailing exhaust
Suspension failure
Heavy G-force
Air streaker
Streamline aerodynamics
Slingshot overtake
Flaming missile
Tumbling crasher
Smoking spinner
Pit stop
Climatic racing
Twisty Monaco
Tight street circuits
Wide race circuits
Flying Finn
Kimi Raikonnen
Jenson Button
Wins in Hungary

Chequered flag
Lewis Hamilton
World Champion
I wanna be
An F1 driver.

Alex Pinfold (12)
Margaret Beaufort Middle School, Riseley

I Have A Dream

I have a dream
That poverty doesn't exist
And everyone is not ridiculously poor or rich
That everyone is equal
And no one is greater than the other

I have a dream
That if someone chooses to be different
We treat them in the same way we wish to be treated
That if someone comes from a different area or country
We ignore their appearance and judge them on their character
                                                               and personality

I have a dream
That people feel confident in sharing
And that their belongings don't get stolen or damaged
That we don't know the meaning of terrorism or war
And all of the countries unite themselves and become one.

I have a dream
That all people acknowledge other's religions
In the way they acknowledge their own
That people respect other's thoughts
And that everyone is right in their own way.

Ryan Bullock (13)
Margaret Beaufort Middle School, Riseley

I Have A Dream

I have a dream . . .
That racism will stop
And the difficulties with violence
Will go away
That both black and white
Will be equal

I have a dream . . .
That everyone can live in peace
That no matter how fat
Or thin you are
We'll always be the same

I have a dream . . .
That there will be no more wars
That people will care
More about the poor
So there will be no more poverty

It would be nice if . . .
My dream would come true
And we could do things
To help the world
Become a better place.

Olivia Jackson (12)
Margaret Beaufort Middle School, Riseley

My Dream

I have a dream to go and ski,
To be a lawyer and see palm trees,
To go to Hong Kong,
Eat Chinese,
To travel the world,
Experience no more debris,
I have a dream for things to change.

Molly Nicholls (12)
Margaret Beaufort Middle School, Riseley

I Have A Dream!

I have a dream that one day there will be no war.
>No war!

I have a dream that one day bullying will stop.
>Stop!

I have a dream that one day children that have been abused will stand up and say, 'Stop!'
>Stop!

I have a dream that one day there will be no poverty.
>No poverty!

I have a dream that one day there will be freedom of speech for everyone.
>Everyone!

I have a dream that one day we can all live in peace and harmony.
>Harmony!

I have a dream that one day we will all have the same equal rights.
>Equal rights!

I have a dream today!

Charlotte Furneaux (13)
Margaret Beaufort Middle School, Riseley

Pointless Cruelty

I have a dream,
That all creatures will be treated equally to Man
Whether they're from the sea, Earth or sky.

I have a dream,
That slaughterhouses will crumble, abandoned by Man,
That fishing boats will be destroyed, along with cruelty.

I have a dream.

Emily May (12)
Margaret Beaufort Middle School, Riseley

Martin Luther King

I wish

I know poverty can end
Only if everyone helps
But some people won't
But I have a wish

I wish poverty would end
I wish that everyone
Would be treated the same,
Not depending on the colour
Of their skin

I wish that all wrongs
Would change to rights
And that's my Utopia
And in my Utopia
All my wishes will come true

That's in Utopia
But in this world
All I can wish for
Is for my wishes to come true.

Max Taylor
Margaret Beaufort Middle School, Riseley

The Spinning Top

My dream,
I have a dream for peace;
With no wars, we can live happily;
I have a dream to mend the world
So nobody will die unnaturally;
All this for me . . .
Peace
And
Harmony.

Elsie Sturton (11)
Margaret Beaufort Middle School, Riseley

I Have A Dream

I have a dream
That one day all fighting and violence will stop
and the world will be at peace,
and all guns, knives and any other weapon will be destroyed.

I have a dream
That racism and bullying will stop
and we will all hold hands in friendship.

I have a dream.

I have a dream
That our sons and daughters will live in harmony
and won't live in fear of war and destruction.

I have a dream
That animal cruelty will stop
and people will treat other people with kindness and respect.

I have a dream
That the world will be a place of kindness and happiness,
where disease, poverty, war and hatred will drift away.

I have a dream.

Tim Palmer (13)
Margaret Beaufort Middle School, Riseley

We Broke Our Promise

We broke our promise,
How can we live with ourselves?

We broke our promise,
What shall we do?

We've lost God's trust,
How could we do that?

Poverty, wars, pollution and waste,
What have we done to this place?

Liam Beckwith & Jordan Nicholson (13)
Margaret Beaufort Middle School, Riseley

Show Us

Show us,
Show us a world where sexism is no more,
And where racism has gone out the door.

Show us,
Show us a world where everyone is equal,
Not a play, not a movie, not even a sequel.

Show us,
Show us where we can all hide,
Not push different colour or sex to the side.

Show us,
Show us how we should treat one another,
Not trip or kill our little sister or brother.

Show us,
Show us how we can treat our life,
Not sit and wait for Grim and his scythe.

Teach us,
Teach us how to look after people,
As if we are one and we are equal.

Jack Hunter (12) & Dean Watson (13)
Margaret Beaufort Middle School, Riseley

I Have A Dream

I have a dream that one day bullying will stop.
                              Stop!

I have a dream that one day there will be no more poverty.
                                        Poverty!

I have a dream that one day children will never be abused.
                                        Abused!

I have a dream that all diseases will be cured.
                              Cured!

Laura Regan (13)
Margaret Beaufort Middle School, Riseley

I Have A Dream

I have a dream . . .
That racism and violence will stop,
That bullying and abuse will stop for children and adults,
And that everyone will be equal, no matter what colour skin they have.

I have a dream . . .
That no matter how fat or skinny you are, people will accept it.
That there will be no more wars and fighting
And everyone will live in peace
And there will be no more bombing in the world.

I have a dream . . .
That everyone can be nice to each other
And no one will bully or hurt anyone or anything.

My dream is made up . . .
From things that we should do
To help the world and help people.

It would be nice if the world was a better place
But usually dreams don't come true!

Olivia Francis (12)
Margaret Beaufort Middle School, Riseley

I Have A Dream

Brothers and sisters unite hand in hand
Family under the sun
Black and white with toes in the sand
Actually having fun
Racism must stop
Earth and the ocean, calm and still
Or all faith in peace will drop
Our half empty glasses must fill
For ourselves to feel real peace
All racism must cease.

Lizzie Moor (12)
Margaret Beaufort Middle School, Riseley

I Have A Dream

I have a dream where I am a superhero

I have a dream I can fly to escape PE

I have a dream where I am invisible to make maths more interesting

I have a dream where I can read minds,
he's head bobbing and it's just too funny

I have a dream where I have super speed,
so I can feed the cat before she bites me

I have a dream where I am super strong,
this way I can fight my sister off the computer

I have a dream where I am flexible enough
to do that move from TV

I have a dream to make food by clicking my fingers,
my dad's cooking isn't that great

I have a dream I can stop time
. . . tick . . . tick . . . tick . . .

Bryanna Harding (12)
Margaret Beaufort Middle School, Riseley

Crimes

It's a crime
It's vandalism to do graffiti
Dropping litter is very bad
And it makes the environment very sad
Oh, it's a crime!

Stealing isn't very good
I don't think your parents steal any food
It's not very clever, it's not very good
I don't even think your friends would
Yes, it's a crime!

Jordan Johnston (11)
Margaret Beaufort Middle School, Riseley

I Have A Dream

I have a dream,
That the train of poverty will grind to a halt,
That the plane of pollution will land,
That injustice will be imprisoned.

I have a dream,
That the poor are loved and cared for,
That the hungry are fed,
That the ill are treated without charge.

I have a dream,
That litter goes in the bin,
That fuel emissions are reduced,
That we act to sustain our existence.

I have a dream,
That the innocent are free,
That the guilty are punished fairly,
That every view is heard and valued.

I have a dream!

Liam Henderson (13)
Margaret Beaufort Middle School, Riseley

The Right Light

We shouldn't have to flee
We should all be free
This isn't a game
We're all the same

Will there ever be a bright light
Or will we just be filled with fright?
Can't just one person see
We're not that different, you and me?

This can't be right
Just because some aren't white.

Polly Witherick (11)
Margaret Beaufort Middle School, Riseley

I Have A Dream

Freedom
      Yes!
Brothers and sisters
            Free!
Together
      Black and white!
Equal
      Always!
Family
      Together!
Dream
      Now!
            For black and white people to share the world and be happy,

Dream - for everyone to have equal rights,

Dream - for an equal world for black children to grow up in,

Dream - for black and white people to get along,

Dream - for a world we all share and get on well in.

Nathan Tennant (11)
Margaret Beaufort Middle School, Riseley

I Have A Dream

I have a dream
that black people will not be judged by their skin
but by their character

I have a dream
of peace and freedom in this world

I have a dream
of equal rights in this world and one nation

I have a dream.

Jack Johnson (12)
Margaret Beaufort Middle School, Riseley

Today, Tomorrow

Today there is racism,
bullying and abuse . . .
I wish tomorrow these
things will not exist.

Today there is war,
blood and fighting . . .
I wish tomorrow these
things will not exist.

Today there is hate,
cruelty and violence . . .
I wish tomorrow these
things will not exist.

Today we have dreams,
but tomorrow these
dreams could be
our future . . .

Sappho Holland (12)
Margaret Beaufort Middle School, Riseley

A Simple Note

I sat for such a
Long
    Long
        Long
            Long
Time under the oak,
Dreaming of the future,
Dreaming of change,
Dreaming of equal
Rights for everyone.

I love to dream.
Do you?

Emily Woodhead (12)
Margaret Beaufort Middle School, Riseley

I Wish

I wish
That racism will finish,
That everyone will walk hand-in-hand,
And stand together proudly.

I wish
That no one will hold a grudge,
That wars will end
And we can unite.

I wish
That people will think about the environment,
Stop killing so many animals
And that we stop littering and recycle.

I wish
That we can walk together,
Without people judging one another,
And make this world a better place.

Gemma Fensham (12)
Margaret Beaufort Middle School, Riseley

I Have A Dream

One day, I hope we will all be equal.
        Equal.

One day, I hope we will not be parted by
an invisible wall.
        Peace to all.

One day, I hope there will be one big crunch
and racism will be gone.
        It's wrong

One day, I hope people will respect each other
and stop the bullies and racism.
        Everybody listen.

Tia Carroll (13)
Margaret Beaufort Middle School, Riseley

I Have A Dream

In my world,
A world of freedom,
A land of peace,
Sorrow and racism fade away.
All people are created equal.

In our kingdom,
A world of freedom,
A land of peace,
Let brotherhood reign.

On our planet,
A world of freedom,
A land of peace,
We sing together

In harmony,
Equal forever.

Alexander Dimmock (12)
Margaret Beaufort Middle School, Riseley

I Have A Dream

I have a dream
That black and white will be equal
Racism will stop
And we'll live in a world of peace

I have a dream
That cruelty will come to a halt
Give more money to the needy
And no wars will ever start.

I have a dream
That hopefully my dream will come true
Live in love and hope
Will the world ever change?

Francesca Graham (11)
Margaret Beaufort Middle School, Riseley

I Have A Dream

I have a dream
Or so it seems
That freedom is the word
With families around the world
And we'll all be equal one day.

We'll not be judged
By skin or colour
But today the nation
Will join together
And we'll all be equal one day.

I have a dream
Or so it seems
That freedom is the word
With families around the world
And we'll all be equal one day.

Gemma Woodhead (11)
Margaret Beaufort Middle School, Riseley

Ethiopia

I watch, I hear
People dying everywhere
What can they do?
What if it was you?

They're hungry and starving,
They're dying, they're dying,
What should they do?
What if it was you?

The ground is completely bare
It is really not fair
What will they do?
Will it ever be you?

Becky Telling (12)
Margaret Beaufort Middle School, Riseley

We'll Soon Be Free

Determination shines above us all;
Pessimism hath not effect;
If God doth say, justice will be done.

The dream I have is of faultless hope;
Its absence shown, a flailing faultless fall;
Its future blows its breath upon a wish.

Wish of wishes entwining into whole;
Whole life crawling from our ginger grasp;
Strengthening hour by hour of human thought.

Though evil persists to keep on harder pressing;
Its cause daunting yet somehow not disturbing;
Prolong our eternal faultless effort.

Let freedom ring from every hill and highway.
We'll soon be free; we'll soon be free!

Mark Willey (13)
Margaret Beaufort Middle School, Riseley

A Simple Man's Dream

The dream of one peaceful man
Suddenly came true
That racism and cruelty would come to a ban
Now the world is so new.
There is no racism, not in this country anymore
We all care for black people
We all look at the same door
Now we can all meet in the same part of the steeple.
We all look like sisters and brothers.
Everyone was racist back then
And cruel to our mothers.
Now look at the way we treat black men
The world is so new.
A better place for me and you.

Natasha Fensome (11)
Margaret Beaufort Middle School, Riseley

Don't Stop Trying

(Inspired by the Martin Luther King 'I Have a Dream' speech)

I believe that equal rights,
Will bring an end to all the fights,
Not all is that our hopes are flying,
To all believers, don't stop trying.

My thoughts are that, we change this place,
To be united as one faith,
When all our luck, is not buying,
To all believers, don't stop trying.

When finally we can be a herd,
The sounds of freedom will be heard,
We shall not hear the unfair sighing,
To all believers, don't stop trying.

Mark Cooper (12)
Margaret Beaufort Middle School, Riseley

I Have A Dream

I have a dream . . .
That people will not be judged by the colour of their skin,
That the train of poverty will grind to a halt,
And the plane of equality will land

I have a dream . . .
That all wars are stopped
That peace will ring out
And there will be no terror strikes

I have a dream . . .
That all people are free
That children can go to school with other races
And there will be no power to certain people

I have a dream that my dream will come true.

Tom Walton (12)
Margaret Beaufort Middle School, Riseley

I Have A Dream

I have a dream
Which I haven't yet seen
That we are all equal
Instead of being evil.

I want freedom
And I will lead them
What is wrong with the world?
We know how to care for others.

We should all care
Because it's not nice, we don't care
What is the matter with this world?
What is the matter with this world?

This is my dream.

Louis Gibson (12)
Margaret Beaufort Middle School, Riseley

I Have A Dream

I have that dream
Everyone will be equal
And people won't be racist.

I have a dream
Black and white men
Will be able to work together in harmony.

I have a dream
There will be peace throughout
The world and weapons will be used
For good not bad.

It will make us all happy.
I really need help to make
My dream change to reality.

Olivia Smith (12)
Margaret Beaufort Middle School, Riseley

Racism In Britain

Racism is still around today,
Is there a solution?
We hope that it will go away,
We have to turn to evolution,
It has to stop right now,
We have to walk away and ignore it,
Everyone wants this, but how?
We've nearly got the hit,
We all have a dream,
That one day this will disappear,
We should all become one team,
So that racism is not near,
Racism should come to a halt,
Racism is society's fault!

Arpan Sekhon (13)
Margaret Beaufort Middle School, Riseley

Racism In Britain

Racism is still around today,
Is there a solution?
We hope that it will go away,
We have to turn to evolution,
It has to stop right now!
We have to walk away and ignore it,
Everyone wants this, but how?
We've nearly got the hit,
Some people just don't think,
Before they do their actions,
They just have to blink,
At people's reactions,
It will all go away one day,
But for now we have to keep it at bay!

Daniel Spiers (13)
Margaret Beaufort Middle School, Riseley

They Had A Dream, Now We Do Too

They had a dream . . .

To stop racism and let the black people of yesterday
be united with the white people of today.

We have a dream . . .

To stop war and resolve our disagreements with words
not guns, with compromise not tanks
and with peace not blackmail.

They will have a dream . . .

That pollution will stop and fuel will be plentiful,
that cancer will be cured and an icon of the past.

Eden Crawley (13)
Margaret Beaufort Middle School, Riseley

War

Why is there war?
    Why?
Why did they make guns?
    Why?
Why do innocent people have to risk their lives?
    Why?
Why do people hurt each other?
    Why?
Why are there fights in the street?
    Why?
Why are people always getting killed?
    Why?

Peter Feneley (12)
Margaret Beaufort Middle School, Riseley

I Have A Dream

That crime and violence stop
and the world is left in peace

I have a dream . . .
that every animal has no cruelty
and every animal has respect

I have a dream . . .
that everybody should be equal
and should not be judged by the colour of their skin.

I have a dream . . .
that we live in peace forever and ever.

Lucy Bates (12)
Margaret Beaufort Middle School, Riseley

My Lovely Family

I have a dream to have a family,
And will grow up and live in harmony.
I will have a baby, Charlie,
We will stay up and party nightly,
But we will always be tidy.
We will always stay and stick with each other
Forever and ever.
But when I die, I will always remember
The good times we had together.

Gabrielle Kyreacou (11)
Margaret Beaufort Middle School, Riseley

One Day

I have a dream
That one day we'll live in a nation
Where we will not be judged by our skin.
The true meaning of life is that all men were created equal.
I have a dream today
That the crooked places will become straight
And rough places will be made straight
And the nation will be united together.
We are all brothers and sisters.

Ben Hoogstraten (12)
Margaret Beaufort Middle School, Riseley

I Have A Dream

I have a dream
All people should be treated equally
No more people getting into fights
The rough places will be made plain
I have a dream
All children should have freedom and play together
No one should be judged by their skin
All that matters is the content of character
I have a dream today.

Anya Luka-Langley (12)
Margaret Beaufort Middle School, Riseley

Freedom

People's skin colour doesn't matter - we're all together.
It will stay like this forever.
Crooked places now will stay straight
Where there used to be hate.

Oliver Stokoe (12)
Margaret Beaufort Middle School, Riseley

Questions

Skin
If black people are judged by it, why aren't white?

Why
If one of the most important people on Earth is black,
and treated with respect,
why aren't all black people?

People
People can change, they just don't want to.

Kitty Rowland (11)
Margaret Beaufort Middle School, Riseley

I Have A Dream

I have a dream
That I want to see
A change in our lives
To stop killings with knives

I want a change!
I want to lock it up in a cage
It can get worse
I want to get rid of thirst.

Ollie King (11)
Margaret Beaufort Middle School, Riseley

He Had A Dream

He had a dream and it came true,
But he did not live to see it bloom,
That black and white would live together,
Let this last forever and ever!

His dream was that of a united nation,
That we would all be equal as God's creations,
That his children would be unjustly judged never,
Let this last forever and ever.

Tilly Rubens (12)
Margaret Beaufort Middle School, Riseley

I Have A Dream

I have a dream that black people will not be judged
But only by what they are deep down.

I have a dream that wars and cruelty will end
And fighting and racism will come to a stop.

I have a dream that bullying will stop
And everyone will live in peace and tranquillity
where bad is no longer around.

Jade Barnes (12)
Margaret Beaufort Middle School, Riseley

Would They?

If white people were black, would they be treated the same?
                              Would they?

If black people were famous, would they be stars?
                              Would they?

If black men ran for president, would anyone get in?
                              Would they?

Zach Witherick (11)
Margaret Beaufort Middle School, Riseley

I *Habbo* Dream

I Habbo dream . . . That the wilderness will come back on Runescape.
I Habbo dream . . . That the multiplayer gaming world will be rid of noobs.
I Habbo dream . . . That Space Station 13 will crash in my back garden.
I Habbo dream . . . That I will hack Lost Witness.

Jonathan Hargreaves (12)
Margaret Beaufort Middle School, Riseley

Vampires

With skin like ice-cold granite,
The colour of a snowy day.
They have eyes as red as deep, dark blood,
Or as gold as flames of fire;
This would be my dream.

They entice you with those eyes,
Making you melt inside.
One step closer . . .
You could be drained of life.
Those eyes and skin,
They draw you in,
This is my dream.

They move as though they are lightning in the sky,
And land like a falling star by your side.
Their voice, a whisper on the wind.
The creature comes closer,
An ice-cold kiss on the lips,
A bite on my neck,
The poison is in,
Is it a nightmare?
No, this is my dream.

Amy Henry (15)
Moyles Court School, Ringwood

Hong Kong

I have a dream . . . to live in the country of my ancestors, Hong Kong.
Whenever I go there, I don't want to return.
Hong Kong makes me happy and I feel at home.

A land of contrasts;
Its famous skyline of tall towers,
Squashed into a tiny area making an exciting, noisy, bustling city.
Traffic always moving, city never sleeping.

A night-time of glittering lights.
A sky filled with the glow from the city.
All against a background of mountains and sea.
Advertisements twinkling in different colours.

Its quiet and peaceful parks with pagodas and delicate bridges
Over calm lakes.
Pink blossom falling like snow onto grassy banks.
People sitting, smiling, enjoying the warm sunshine.

Fluffy clouds passing over towering mountains
Against a bright blue sky.

Streets full of food stalls with sizzling crispy duck.
Crunchy fried snacks of prawns and dumplings.
Everyone tempted by the delicious flavours.
Carrying trays of all sorts of delights.

The aroma of delicious sauces fills the air.

Colourful parades of pretty Chinese girls in pink silk and satin.
Black smooth hair and red lips.
Slim girls in beautiful dresses swaying slowly through the city streets.
Laughing children dressed in amazing costumes smile and dance
As the parade goes by.
Busy people rushing to work, cars and trams filling the streets.
Everyone seeming to know where they're going, no one stopping
To stand and stare.

I have a dream . . . to work in Hong Kong,
To be successful and wealthy
Enjoy seeing my relations, aunty, uncle and cousins.

Kim Chung (14)
Moyles Court School, Ringwood

'Twas Back Two Years

'Twas back two years from now, that I finally came upon to see,
that our gruelling, testing journey would be so very long;
exasperatingly, excruciatingly so; blood and sweat would emerge -
that task was ours to keep . . .
. . . that one way out, one ticket, one chance, the one way street and track,
'twas like we were behind a dark building,
unable to enter our full bloom for the time being.

At the early dawn of the moist and dewy October day back two years from
now, a group of us, seven to start for the first year,
formed; but only three of us knew each other,
to have four unknown players on the football pitch un-met,
would be another thing.

Our name was on the team's new blue and black bag, that was not totally
clean, containing only the team's shirts, Man of the Match trophy and the
crumpled red folder of future fixtures.
We were now a team for one, three or even four years, together;
to lose week after week took its toll on us, all of us, each and every one of
us, and also was humiliatingly long.
The new fresh grass was lush and sweet. If only we knew.

So as we sank down the tables, we lost heaps of original glory and dreams:
though we had never shared any of them between us aloud
so for the rest of the season we practiced on the eve of Thursdays
and played for a couple o' games on the dawn of the Saturdays.

But the one soul that I haven't mentioned, is our faithful manager, Andrew,
expecting to drop his son off at his new team, then manager in an instant,
in a flash; he trained us, helped us, the whole group became better at the
beautiful game of football,
and towards the end of our first season together - the results came in, thick
and fast, every single Saturday.

And to tell you all the truth, we came off the bottom, with one single point of the drop, we were now a proper soccer team, working as a team, with all the fan support we could ever need;
we had all found our riches and combined them as one.
To think that all could have been in vain without our manager, Andrew Dawson; we expect to win, we want to win, we shake our heads when we have played a bad game, or lost. This is us now.

With players all helping out, and with me the skipper and main defender, and Andrew on the line, our manager two years on, our guide, who helps us with anything and everything, any time at all.
These are the ups and downs of our Saturday morning team.

Alex Parkinson (12)
Moyles Court School, Ringwood

I Have A Dream

I had a dream I saw a light, the bright moon lighting up
the cold street.
A person in a black coat came out of the light.

I said, 'What do you want? Who are you?'
He replied in his deep masculine voice, 'I am the one
you have been looking for.'

His wavy brown hair came out of the coat
and his face became familiar.
It was Aaron Johnson, the young actor that had millions of fans
screaming over him.

I couldn't believe it, it was the person I had wanted to meet,
my hero!

He smiled at me and took my hand
I said, 'Why are you here?'
He replied, 'I have been looking for you and I love you.'

I smiled and felt like the most amazing thing had happened.
But then I woke up and it was a dream, not just any dream,
the best dream!

Emily Cooke (15)
Moyles Court School, Ringwood

Think

Think . . .
Of a day without any sun.
Think . . .
Of a sea without any water.
Think . . .
Of a land without any colour.
Think . . .
Of a night without any stars!
Think . . .
Of a school without any children.
Think . . .
Of a child without any laughter.
Think . . .
Of a surfer without any waves.
Think . . .
Of a town without any people!
Think . . .
Of music without any notes.
Think . . .
Of a fire without any heat.
Think . . .
Of a forest without any trees.
Think . . .
Of a world without any animals!
Think . . .
Of a plant without any life.
Think . . .
Of a book without any words.
Think . . .
Of a life without any joy.
Think . . .
Of a life without any life!

Think about what you're doing
To the whole world.

Live your life right.

Anna Patterson (11)
Moyles Court School, Ringwood

Anne

I have a dream,
That we don't have to hide.

I have a dream,
That I don't have to put up with her.

I have a dream,
That my friends will be safe.

I have a dream,
That Daddy will get better.

I have a dream,
That I can have my own room.

I have a dream,
That they'll stop treating me like an infant.

I have a dream,
That the air raids will stop,
So I can sleep at night.

I have a dream,
That one day I will smell fresh air again!

I have a dream,
That *he* loves me.

I have a dream,
That we'll be out of here soon.

I have a dream,
That the police do not discover us.

I have a dream,
That we never have to hear, smell
Or see that awful place.

I have a dream,
That my diary never ends.

Yours,
   Anne.

Alice Clark (15)
Moyles Court School, Ringwood

The Sea

I am a fish. Nothing special.
I'm not a clown or an angel.
My scales barely shine.
Yet, I live in a cavern of hope,
A treasure trove full of beauty wherever you look.
The sea. So vast, so deep, so amazing.

I often wonder,
What magnificent things must lurk in the dark,
In the murky depths where no fish dare go.
How many wonders remain undiscovered down there?
Are there demons down there in the black?

I look out. Coral reefs scatter the floor,
Seaweed claws at the rippling surface, but never reaches,
Tied down by its roots.
A shower of my friends are rushing towards me.
I wonder what is happening.
They yell, 'Shark! Shark on the horizon!'

Over the rocks a black shape moves.
It swims into the light and it bares its teeth.
From where it's come, blood pollutes the water.
The seaweed cowers as the shark swims by,
Yet, dirt is still flicked into the abyss,
Now the water is murky and dark.
The all too common stench of blood fills the water.

All in that moment, the cavern of beauty has changed.
Now all I see is blood, death.

I am a fish.
I live in a cave of disaster
A treasure trove full of death wherever you look.
The sea. So vast, so deep, so terrible.

Douglas Murdoch (13)
Moyles Court School, Ringwood

I Have A Dream

I dream of flowers, I dream of trees and sometimes
I dream of scary things
The dreams I seem to remember are the ones about terrible things that
worry me a lot.

I have a dream when I am asleep, when I am awake I can't remember what
it was.
I dream of monsters creeping in the forest,
making noises in the woods.

I dream of the sun going up and down every morning
and every night
I hear creepy noises in the night.
I hear the wildlife, animals munching on food.

In the morning I hear bees buzzing around
I hear the birds singing in the morning
I hear the trees wafting around every morning.

I dream of flowers growing as high as they possible can go
and living for a long time.
I dream of saving the poor and helping them,
I dream that I could fly higher than anybody else
and higher than the sky.

I have a dream of the world turning inside out and upside down
I dream of the bad people going to a different planet.

I have a dream of saving the world and helping other people live
I dream of this world, helpful and happy with no violence and cruelty in it.

I have a dream of no bullies and horrible people
I have a dream of no murders in this world.

I dream of kindness and everybody is happy
and not afraid of this planet.

Lauren Palmer (11)
Moyles Court School, Ringwood

Dream Of Seasons

I dream of beautiful colours,
I dream of browns, oranges and yellows,
I dream of the trees shedding their leaves
Like an animal shedding its fur.
I dream of leaves being crunched underfoot,
I dream of walks in the forest,
I dream of rainbows,
I dream of autumn.

I dream of winter wonderlands,
I dream of cold, crisp mornings,
I dream of Jack Frost,
I dream of Christmas,
I dream of snowballs,
I dream of a new year,
I dream of winter.

I dream of birds singing,
I dream of baby animals being born,
I dream of children playing,
I dream of preparing for summer,
I dream of sunsets getting later,
I dream of the smell of freshly cut grass,
I dream of spring.

I dream of sunbathing,
I dream of sunsets,
I dream of swimming,
I dream of a peaceful ocean,
I dream of golden beaches,
I dream of summer.

I dream of dreams.

Anna Peachey (16)
Moyles Court School, Ringwood

What If?

What if the world had no colour,
Flowers had no scent,
And bees had no sting?

What if the sun had no light,
People didn't have babies,
And teachers had no knowledge?

What if people had no food,
Seasons didn't change,
And animals had no life?

Would I be alive today
If those phrases were true?

What if everyone had a home,
People didn't die,
And neither creature nor human ever suffered?

What if we could cure all diseases,
People got help when they needed it,
And everyone had an education?

If the sea had no water,
And the wind had no breeze,
People had no tongues,
And I wasn't loved?

What if I spoke and nobody understood?
I was a leader and no one followed?
I lived and no one knew?

Would I be alive today,
If those phrases were true?

Khlöe Smith (12)
Moyles Court School, Ringwood

Seasons

I have a dream in the spring
Of flowers starting to bloom
In the flowers I see butterflies
So colourful like bright green trees
The trees have many bright coloured leaves
All the branches weaving in and out
With nests carefully made out of twigs.

I have a dream in summer
Of the sun shining brightly over us
All the bees come out of hiding
To start to make our delicious honey
The honey is as gold as a piece of jewellery
From the honey I think of ice cream
Cold and sweet.

I have a dream in the autumn
Of all the leaves turning red
The red leaves turn into fire
For Bonfire Night people gather around the fire
Eating toffee apples and drinking warm hot chocolate
The toffee apples are as sticky as glue in-between your hands
Up above there are giant-sized fireworks.

I have a dream in the winter
People getting ready for the arrival of Christmas
Children helping put up decorations and going out with their parents
To buy their friends and family presents
Christmas comes, everyone is having fun with the family
Christmas ends and New Year's Day arrives, and the year starts over again.

Jasmine Kingsley-Cole (11)
Moyles Court School, Ringwood

Free

I'm trapped, I can't escape,
My world is small,
The walls are closing in,

I'm scared,

I can't go on like this,
I must go on through,
I have to have faith,
The shackles that hold me down,
Will break if I have faith,

As the light fades,
I cry out with fear,
There are no doors or windows,
I feel like I'm going to die alone,

I have faith,

Though at the very moment that it is the worst
Light floods the chambers,
A door appears,
I stand, I reach,

I open the door, I run . . .
I run away as fast as I can,

Wild horses gallop by,
Birds fly above,
Rabbits run with me,

I am free.

Meredith Jones (13)
Moyles Court School, Ringwood

I Had A Dream!

Last night I had a dream,
Unlike any other dream,
It was like a never-ending story,
Full of magical tales.

It started off dark and dull,
But it became so bright and beautiful,
And in front of my eyes, I couldn't believe it,
Angels appeared before me.

The scene changed yet again,
The angels still were there,
But I found myself on a country road, in spring.
I felt so alive, so free by what I could see.

The birds gathered around and began to sing,
It was indeed the most beautiful thing,
The deer came through,
As I saw them smile I knew this was where I belonged.

In my dream I travelled far,
It's kinda scary not knowing where you are,
Up the mountains, through the trees,
The angels still flying behind me.

Then I thought I heard one say,
'Come on, wake up, it's school today,'
When I opened my eyes I was in my room,
And it was no angel, just my mum with a broom.

Charlotte Eldon (10)
Moyles Court School, Ringwood

Fame

Fame

Fame . . . is a powerful word
Some see it for money
Some see it for satisfaction, maybe even pride
I see it as a hard ambition that people take for life!

Fame

Some see it to gain power
Some see it to be recognised
Some gain it, some lose it
I will always win it!

Fame

Is all about taking chances in life
Taking that jump
And living the reality
That is what fame counts for!

Fame

So go on
Take that jump
With both arms open
While you have this one and only chance
Never, ever look back!

Danny Whitelock (15)
Moyles Court School, Ringwood

Evolution

I believe in evolution because it makes sense.
The idea of what comes next is really rather immense!
To think we come from apes and life started in the sea!
It often makes me wonder how I ever became me.

Spencer Jones (11)
Moyles Court School, Ringwood

My World

The sound of waves fill the air
Like a calm sea storm.
The sand feels soft beneath my feet
It's like walking on clouds.
No one is here except for me and Jess
It's as if everybody has disappeared.
My dog runs across the sand
Flipping the sand behind him,
The more he runs
The more sand flies into the air
I feel happy and not worried
Though I know this dream will have to end
And the sand will become hard gravel
And the sea will become screams of terror
Because that is our world
Cold, full of terror and full of sadness.
Though I know that life isn't mine
Because sand would become soft sheets
And the sea would be my dog,
Yes, my dog
Snoring and scratching his bed
As if he was running after rabbits
Because that is *my* world.

Jasmine West (11)
Moyles Court School, Ringwood

Heroes Among Men

They were heroes among men,
They were brave and determined,
They were used as weapons,
But maintained their dignity,
They fought for us, many gave their lives,
They were heroes among men.

Now they live together in big houses,
Trying to recall their glory days,
They find it hard to feed or dress themselves,
They sit and look at one another,
Trying to think how their lives ended up this way,
They were heroes among men.

They are not acknowledged or respected,
They had a year's worth of thanks,
But now they are forgotten,
Take the time to look into their eyes;
Courage, bravery and valour will shine through,
They were heroes among men.

They used their lives to fight for our free living,
We are abusing this freedom. Is this fair?
They truly are heroes among men.

Becky Brown (16)
Moyles Court School, Ringwood

I Have A Dream

I have a dream that I can stop global warming.
I have a dream that I can stop the drug dealings
and all the murders.
I have a dream that I can stop all the bombers.
I have a dream that I can stop all the missing children from going
                                   missing or being taken away.
So my dream is about stopping darkness and bringing lightness.

Zahra Hall (11)
Moyles Court School, Ringwood

A Dream In Reality

In reality it would mean perfection
An achievement
A goal
One aim in life
Picked off the list of 'to dos'!
My dream is simple
Gives others pride and is a powerful ability
A fortunate adage to my personality
A gleam in the distance
When I am sad
My dream overwhelms me
If only I could
It would be so perfect
Such a wonderful opportunity
For me to show everybody
I'm not a little girl
I'm a lady
I have a voice
I want to use it
My dream is to sing
It is a real dream
And as real as me!

Megan Victoria Price (16)
Moyles Court School, Ringwood

Summer

The sound of summer's sizzling BBQ!
Sausages frying in the pan.
A symphony of voices chattering
The air now filled with laughter
And the sweet perfume of roses swaying in the breeze.
As cameras click and freeze that moment to store
In our memories as we all head home for autumn.

Alex Wood (11)
Moyles Court School, Ringwood

I Have A Dream

I have a dream that one day we will explore the deepest
parts of space
I have a dream that everyone will work as one to explore space
I have a dream that everyone should be equal and only a few
should lead us as a race
My dream could have been reality by now
We could have been to Mars by now but it stopped at the moon
There is so much that is unexplored
Soon the only way that it could happen is that people need to see
the beauty of space
Everyone wants to be an individual or part of some group
That's why we haven't got to Mars or Pluto yet
If we don't, we'll be trapped and we might even destroy Earth
On Earth everyone is a mountain and has their own ambitions
But when we explore enough space
The mountains won't be as crowded on Earth
Other species might exist as well, similar to us
Then the human race can be worthy of the universe
and have universal respect
This won't happen if the big leaders of the world see a bigger beauty of
space
Those leaders could make this dream a reality.

Luke Stevens (14)
Moyles Court School, Ringwood

I Have A Dream

I have many dreams
I have many ambitions
Some are real and some are fake
I know that I will never play football professionally
But I know one day I will have the chance to go to Hawaii and surf
So some dreams are real
And some dreams are fake
Then why have the fake ones?
I think the fake ones are the dreams
Dreams you know probably will not come true
And the real ones are ambitions and things you would like to do
Only the really lucky people live their dreams
However a lot of people do a lot of the things they want to do
The people whose dreams come true
Are the people who believe the dreams are not fake
When I was young I dreamt I would play professional football
And I really believed I would
As I grew older it became just a dream
A fake ambition. Now it's only a dream
As you get older, ambitions become dreams
As you just don't have the time for them.

Christopher Winrow (16)
Moyles Court School, Ringwood

I Have A Dream

That I can end all wars
And stop people from dying
When I think about what happened in the past
I wonder
What was life like for people my age?

Were they happy?
Did they think about the future?
And here I am in the future now.

Josh Cummings (14)
Moyles Court School, Ringwood

Where Do I Go?

Where do I go to learn apart from school?
Where do I go to find food except for the supermarket?
Where do I go to find shelter apart from a house?
Where do I go to find warmth except for clothes?
These questions have answers.
But do these . . .?
Where do I go to stop the wars?
Where do I go to feed the hungry?
Where do I go to help the injured?
Where do I go to shelter the homeless?
Where do I go to stop the recession?
Where do I go to help those who need help?
Where do I go to rescue the endangered?

Where do I go to save the world?

Where do I go to answer these questions?

Where do I go to find inspiration?

Inspiration comes in all different shapes and forms
My inspiration comes from the world and what's within it.

Aly Davie (12)
Moyles Court School, Ringwood

I Have A Dream

I have a dream that I can fly.
To soar through the air like an eagle.
To be as free as a bird.
Watching everyone below me.

I have a dream to be able to breathe underwater.
To have gills like a fish.
Swimming beneath the surface.
Watching everyone above me.

These are my dreams.

Sam Wilkes (13)
Moyles Court School, Ringwood

Swapping Seasons

The brisk winter is still here,
Wind, rain, sleet and snow.
How I dream for the season to change.

The sun begins to rise,
Upon a still and silent world.
The long-awaited spring months,
Have finally arrived.

The hibernating daffodils start to stretch and wake,
From a cold wintry sleep,
As the warmth from the golden sun,
Begins to caress each flower's petals.

The fields of spiky frosted grass,
Are touched with the glisten from the shining spring sun,
The once stiff, harsh blades are now set free,
From their icy cocoons.

The white encrusted fields,
Become endless acres of rich emerald grass.
How I dream for the season to change.

Charlotte Barna (16)
Moyles Court School, Ringwood

I Can Fly

I can fly, fly away
Fly up high, fly down below
Away I go, away I go
I can fly, I can fly.

I start my journey, off I go
Ducking and diving past the trees
I search for food, looking around
I see my chance and I take that chance
I can fly, I can fly.

Henry Glaister (14)
Moyles Court School, Ringwood

Memories

I have a dream
To take my life in pictures
And never forget a thing
To remember all the good times
That I miss the most

I have a dream
To write my life in words
And all the little details
To describe the amazing moments
That will stay with me forever

I have a dream
To record my life in music
And remember the rhythm
To sing about the memories
That I once had

People can repeat my life if they really want but not these dreams
They are mine.

Rosie Lees (15)
Moyles Court School, Ringwood

I Want To Fly

I dream of flying so high
So very high
So extremely high in the sky.
I dream of flying like a bird
With gigantic wings
Feel the wind on my feathers.
A cool sea breeze,
As I glide by.
That's why I dream of flying
So high
In the treacherous sky.

Diggory Simons (13)
Moyles Court School, Ringwood

My Life, My Dream, My Future

I love my life,
Both ups and downs,
My life is not a mess at all,
I have not failed,
I celebrated my achievements,
And in my exams,
What is there left to do?
Sit here and watch time fly?
Sit here and watch my future crumble?
Never
Not ever,
I will never let my parents down,
I'll pursue my dream,
Fight for it,
And,
When the time comes,
Catch it,
And build the ladder called 'my future'.

Jack Wilson (12)
Moyles Court School, Ringwood

Spring Is In The Air

Shiny emerald buds are bursting for life,
Daffodils and snowdrops wake up,
Dancing like ballerinas in the March winds.

Laced wing flies hover,
Bejewelled butterflies bask on silk pillows,
As bumblebees hum like contented children.

Small animals are stirring from a long winter's sleep,
Peeping out into the diamond daylight.

The crisp air scented with blossom.

This is my dream.

Olivia Argent (10)
Moyles Court School, Ringwood

London 2012

I'd just been entered for the Olympics.
In some of my races I was versing Michael Phelps.
I could not believe it.
I was listening to my iPod on the way there to London.
My hands were shaking like mad.
I had brought all my cereal bars with me.
I checked if I had everything and I did.
I got in the stadium, it was unbelievable!
My first race was the 50 metres freestyle.
I was in the fastest lane, right next to Michael Phelps.
I dived in, the water was cold and I saw the cameras
At the bottom of the pool.
It was pretty cool but my legs were kicking like mad.
I was level with him but then it was the last 25 metres.
I got in front of him and I beat him by a fraction
And I got a new world record.
It was unbelievable!
I sprang into the air, out of the water.

Mikey Kingsley (13)
Moyles Court School, Ringwood

I Have A Dream

I wish those times of loneliness would all disappear.
There's so many around but you're never near
When you're near my heart, I feel no longer alone but so subtle
My love, I feel I am home.
This is what I have been through my whole life
Loneliness, deserted for what I feel's right
So why should they care? For I am happy elsewhere
When he's in my arms I feel no longer alone
But in Heaven where my worries are no more.

Rosie Kerr (15)
Moyles Court School, Ringwood

Andrei Arshavin

He plays like a dream,
He scores lots of goals,
He wears the number 23 on his shirt,
Arshavin is a great player.

He has an amazing shot,
When he scores,
He celebrates in his own way,
Arshavin is a good player.

He has blond hair,
He looks the part,
He is a snappy winger,
Arshavin is a fine player.

He is a skilful player,
He masters the step-over,
And the back heel,
Andrei Arshavin is an excellent player.

Tom Brown (11)
Moyles Court School, Ringwood

Leaving Town

I pack my bags and take one last look at the ground
It has been my home for seven years now
There have been good times and bad times
When I am down and up
But at last I have found peace now
I make my way across vast areas
To find my final destination in which I will
Take my last few years with everlasting love
And pass on my knowledge through my blood
As I take my last few breaths I rekindle my past
Through vast valleys and open plains
But still just to be left to the boatman rain.

Robert Fraser (15)
Moyles Court School, Ringwood

I Had A Dream

I had a dream that spring had arrived,
I had a dream that the daffodils had bloomed,
I had a dream that the grass had grown and spring had come,
I had a dream that we were sitting in a tree
And watching the world go by,
I had a dream that the sun was beating down
And the animals had come out of hibernation,
I had a dream that the chicks had hatched,
The dream changed from bleak to expectation,
The dream came from bleak to bloom,
Through the wind cold and grey,
The happiness that Easter brings!
I had a dream about the bunny rabbits hopping
And the Easter eggs with chocolate thick,
There is magic all around us, you can feel it in the air,
For the lovely signs of springtime,
I had a dream that it's a time of fulfilled promise, hope and cheer.

Jade Metcalfe (15)
Moyles Court School, Ringwood

I Have A Dream

I have a dream
That one day war will be over and everybody will live in peace
I have a dream
That bullies will realise what they have done to helpless people
I have a dream
That someone will find a cure for cancer
I have a dream
That all around the world everyone is equal
I have a dream
That people will realise what they are doing to the atmosphere
I have a dream
That all these things will come true.

Florence Radford (11)
Moyles Court School, Ringwood

Blue Waters

My heart sank as I watched the sun go down,
lost on an island, me all alone

I watched the sea settle as I wandered around on the island

I sat and I watched and wondered if there was any hope that
I would be rescued and taken home

The sun disappeared and night had come
I gathered some palm leaves and lay them on the sand

I lay on the sand with my head on the leaves
I closed my eyes and fell asleep.

I heard people calling but thought it was a dream but then
I opened my eyes and saw a ship in the distance

The captain told me they had come to take me home

I whispered to myself with joy
My dream had come true.

Lauren Wright (13)
Moyles Court School, Ringwood

Kids With Guns

What would the world be like if kids had no guns?
The world would probably be more at peace.
No killing, crime, robbery and drive-bys.
Just imagine what it would be like.
Not seeing kids walking around with guns
Pointing them at people, threatening that they will shoot.
Citizens begging for mercy!
Just praying to God that hopefully they do not shoot.
Just imagine what it would be like if kids had no guns.

Lloyd Geddis (12)
Moyles Court School, Ringwood

Some People Dream . . .

Some people dream of becoming famous,
To be recognised at every turn they take.

Some people dream of their life in a different perspective,
To be poles apart from whom they really are.

Some people dream of being a superhero,
To fly through the skies and save people's lives.

Some people dream of the future,
For it to be bright, brilliant and beautiful.

Some people dream to open doors in their minds,
To keep the keys to their personal world inside their heads.

Some people dream to escape themselves,
To put up a wall to the world we live in.

Some people dream just because,
Some people dream for no reason at all.

Rachel Lucas (15)
Moyles Court School, Ringwood

I Have A Dream

I have a dream that poverty is ended
That wealth doesn't matter

I have a dream that I become a pro golfer
That every shot I take is applauded by thousands

I have a dream that racism is stopped
That everyone gets equal rights

I have a dream that the recession is over
And more jobs are made

I have a dream that makes our lives like ladders -
Everything we do either gets us up or takes us down

I have a dream.

Scott Jones (14)
Moyles Court School, Ringwood

I Have A Dream

You are such an inspiration to me,
All of the things that you have achieved.
You have helped everyone that needed it,
Been friendly to everyone companionless.

You will go down in history as phenomenal,
You are as wise as an owl!
You're everything I aspire to be,
So thank you for being so wonderful, Mum!

Jade Sax (15)
Moyles Court School, Ringwood

My Mum

My mum
She's always caring for us
Always there to clean the dust
Never makes a fuss.

My mum
She's very understanding
Not the one to be lying
She's always trying.

My mum
Her smile brightens my day
In each and every way.
I love her more and more each day.

My mum
She's one in a million
I wouldn't change her for a billion
She's the one for us
Death till dust.

We love our mum,
She's our best charm.

Amyna Visram (14)
Northolt High School, Northolt

When I Grow Up . . .

When I grow up . . .
I want to be a dentist,
I want to fix people's teeth.

When I grow up . . .
I want to be an architect,
I want to design a lot of buildings.

When I grow up . . .
I want to earn a lot of money,
I want to be rich.

When I grow up . . .
I want to help poor people,
I want to donate money for them.

When I grow up . . .
I want to have my own business,
I want to have a restaurant.

When I grow up . . .
I don't want my parents to work anywhere else,
I want them to be the boss of our own business.

When I grow up . . .
I want to design my own villa,
I want it to have a mixture of Spanish, Italian, Filipino style.

When I grow up . . .
I want to keep in touch with my friends,
Until we have grey hairs.

When I grow up . . .
I want to travel around the world,
I want to visit every country there is.

When I grow up . . .
I want to achieve all of this,
Before I go away and never come back.

Athena Echave (13)
Northolt High School, Northolt

My Inspirational Heroes!

Who inspires you? They inspire me!
My mum inspires me,
By encouraging me.
My mum inspires me,
By supporting me.
My mum inspires me,
By always being there for me in times of need.
My mum inspires me,
As she helps me through miserable times.
My mum inspires me,
As she stays with me even if I demean her.
My mum is one of my idols because . . .
My mum inspires me.

My dad inspires me,
By helping me.
My dad inspires me,
By staying strong when he breaks down inside.
My dad inspires me,
By raising this family.
My dad inspires me,
By the way he lives his life with the surroundings he's with.
My dad inspires me,
As he always gets through rough times.
My dad inspires me,
When he makes me laugh.
My dad inspires me,
When he pulls a face that opposes what he feels inside.
My dad is also one of my cherishing idols because . . .
My dad inspires me.

My sister inspires me,
As she puts up with all her problems and gets through them.
My sister inspires me,
By always being there for me with a shoulder to cry on.
My sister inspires me,
By being brave.
My sister inspires me,
By always reassuring me with a hug and a kiss.
My sister is also one of my treasuring idols because . . .

My sister inspires me.
They all inspire me and are my idols for a special reason,
I don't change an inspirational idol every season.
They believed in me and believed my potential can make a difference,
But I didn't need a reference,
My thoughts themselves could change the world and so could yours.
They all inspire me, but does anyone inspire you?
Does anyone inspire those living in less developed countries to stay awake
a little longer
And try to never let go?
Just think . . .
Could you be the one to make a difference or inspire them?

Janany Sathasivam (14)
Northolt High School, Northolt

Could You Imagine?

Could you imagine . . .
Being taken by the breeze,
Going wherever the wind takes you
Flying with the birds and the bees?

Could you imagine . . .
A world with no fear or doubts
No troubles or worries
Having the children run about?

Could you imagine . . .
The warm rays on your face
Being taken in the moment?
How I dream of this place.

Could you imagine . . .
Throwing away the key
To your hopes and dreams
Trapped forever
Stripped of your pride and dignity?

Daniel Ewusie-Wilson (13)
Northolt High School, Northolt

Two Faces Of Fame

Killed for fame
A peaceful man
Who changed the world
Like not many can

Dropped out of school
Formed a band
Pressured by death
Yet he persevered and . . .

The band surpassed
And led him to fame
All around the world
But then the day came . . .

When he changed his ways
And protested for peace
Speaking his mind
Ordering war to cease

December 1980
Signing autographs for fans
Unaware that one
Was the man . . .

Who moments later
Would call his name
And fire five shots
All for quick fame

He fell to his knees
Trying to speak
But lost consciousness
For being made weak

Covered with a coat
Rushed to hospital
But pronounced dead on arrival
Death was unstoppable

Remember forever
The world allied
For everyone knew

That a great man had died

'My role in society, or any artist's or poet's role, is to try and express what we all feel. Not to tell people how to feel. Not as a preacher, not as a leader, but as a reflection of us all'.
John Lennon
1940-1980.

James Kilduff (14)
Northolt High School, Northolt

Inspiration

Inspiration, inspiration, the start of everything,
Someone could inspire you to do something great.
But do not fret,
If you don't look like them,
If you don't sound like them,
And many more . . .
If you are not like them in any way,
That makes you unique in your own way.
Or
Start a big change, for example Martin Luther King.
He went *'ping'*
And fought for his rights
Your idea could never be too big.
Don't be a pig!
To expect everything to do right
Everybody fails, so, try, try and maybe try again!
Don't give up. I want none of that!
Until you lose all your fat (failure attempts)
With a glorious *thing!*
And that *thing,* could be anything!
Now, it is for you to decide what that *thing* is
I will flow through your eyes, for you to understand,
When you read this poem
And show you where your *thing* lies.

Gowry Ganenthira (13)
Northolt High School, Northolt

They Inspire Me . . .

When they take the stage, they take my breath away
When they take the stage, they take England's breath away
When they take the stage, they take the world's breath away.

Every move they make, makes me want to move more,
Every step they take, makes me want to take more steps
Every turn they make, makes me want to turn like them.

Something as simple as hearing their name,
Puts me in a place which cannot be explained.
I get butterflies in my stomach
When they get ready to blast the stage.
But as soon as they do those butterflies fly away
And my heart opens to them.

They inspire me . . . inspire me to take a chance
A chance that I always dreamt of taking
Right now . . . that chance will never be left untaken.

When they take the stage, they take my breath away,
When they take the stage, they take England's breath away,
When the take the stage, they take the world's breath away.

Super Crew! Super Crew! Super Crew!

They inspire me.

Siham Ali (15)
Northolt High School, Northolt

The Battle!

Look around - what do you see?
Just look around - is it what you want the Earth to be?
Think - how can you make it better?
Just think - by a speech, protest or letter?
Dream - that torture to animals will go away!
Just dream - that it will slowly disappear every day!
Help - animals who get killed for no reason at all!
Just help - or else the world will fall!
Look around - is the place better?
Just look around - did it help with the letter?
Think - could you help us?
Just think - or will you be a speck of dust?
Dream - that we have won!
Just dream - that all our work is done!
Help - give a little thought, that is all we need!
Just help - we need money or no deed!
Look around - have we won?
Just look around - I think we are done!

Kimberley Seaward (14)
Northolt High School, Northolt

Inspiration

I magine a world without war.
N eedless to say just imagine . . .
S ay how you feel when you feel it.
P eace or war, you decide!
I magine a world without poverty.
R ain or sun, make a difference.
A pples for hungry mouths remembered.
T ackle it now.
I magine a world without family.
O h imagine, imagine!
N o, *inspiration* is what you need.

Ryan Butler (14)
Northolt High School, Northolt

Stephen Hawking

Confined to a wheelchair
Isolated from society
Wouldn't it be boring
If there wasn't so much variety?

He didn't sit back and watch
His disability didn't get him down
He spoke his words to the world
Now he's a legend, world renowned.

This was not enough
He wanted to reach greater heights
With the determination on his face
He took a flight right up to space

You may know him for his books
Or maybe on TV
But I can now say one thing . . .
He always will inspire me.

James Ellett (14)
Northolt High School, Northolt

Gangs

Is it really worth it, what is there to gain?
Do you think you could live with it, put up with the shame?
Does it really make you look hard, put you above the rest?
Do you see it as a challenge, merely just a test?
Do you think it's funny, taking someone's life?
So please don't be foolish, just put down the knife!

Do you like the sound of gunshots, is it music to your ears?
Does it bring you pleasure, being the cause of people's tears?
Do you really need to do it, put the bullets in that gun?
Is there actually a reason, or is it just for fun?
So put a stop to this violence, stop all the bloodshed
Just let them be, allow them to sleep tightly in their beds.

Jamie Carpenter (13)
Northolt High School, Northolt

Knife Crime

You hear about it on the news, everyone has personal views.
Walking around, happy as can be, the people always wonder,
Who next it could be.
People die on the streets, it's like news, on a constant repeat.
Kids run riot with knives and guns, showing off and thinking it's fun.
Teens think it's cool to hang with their little bad boy gangs,
Their evil, selfish, cruel minds take people's lives, just like mine.
Innocent, innocent, I did plead, but they didn't bother listening to me.
They stabbed my guts then I did bleed, my heart gave in so suddenly.
Only three words I would have given to describe my awful death,
Blood, sweat and tears
Blood is for the victim, me, who laid helpless and soon dead.
Sweat is for the criminal who ran scared and unled.
Tears are for my family, who cried for the blood that shed.
Oh innocent, oh innocent I did plead, why did these criminals choose me?
A year, a month, a day maybe, then my killer's walking around,
                                        head high, and free.

Katie Conroy (13)
Northolt High School, Northolt

What If . . .?

What if one day you lose someone close?
Suddenly somebody carries a knife
And you've lost the one you love the most.

What if one day everybody lost all hope?
The world becomes so selfish,
It just couldn't cope.

What if one day everyone decided to carry a knife?
You wouldn't be able to walk the streets,
Or live a safe life.

What if we could put an end to it all
Put away the knives, be brave and stand tall?

Charlotte Davies (13)
Northolt High School, Northolt

Live Not Kill

Why did I hear a gunshot?
Why did I hear another person die?
Who will fill his slot?

What did he do to deserve this?
What has his family done?
Why couldn't his mum give him his last kiss?
What have they done to lose a son?

And now you've caused this disaster,
What was the ultimate prize?
Did you enjoy the bit of laughter?
Keep telling yourselves lies,
I can see you made killing your master!

Why did I hear a gunshot?
Why did I hear another person die?
Who will fill this slot?

Ikram Abdulle (14)
Northolt High School, Northolt

If I Could Only Change One Thing . . .

If I could only change one thing
I would make peace for everyone and everything.
There would be no more fighting, lying and dying.

If I could only change one thing
No one would live with fears
There would be no more tears
The whole world would work as a team.

If I could only change one thing
There would be no more killing each other.
It makes no sense.

If I could only I would change one thing
We would all be living the dream.

Max Petty (13)
Northolt High School, Northolt

What Happened?

What happened to the dodos?
Were have they gone?
What's happening to the pandas?
Tell me what went wrong.
What's happening to the rhinos?
Couldn't the species go on?
We're lucky that humans aren't extinct
Otherwise, like the Titanic, the Earth will sink
And all that will be left is a ghost town full of regret.
We would never forget,
It would be engraved on the tombstone of our mind
How we slayed animalkind.
If you could change one thing in life
Would you protest how we treat animals
And save their lives?

Alanna Clarke-Beattie (14)
Northolt High School, Northolt

The Ancient Egyptians

The Egyptians inspire me, do they you?
All the paintings and the pyramids too?
I love the creativity and the architecture,
The tours in the sun, each with a lecture.

Cruises on the Nile, drinking and relaxing,
Along the banks where the crocodiles sit,
Cairo and the towns, places without taxing,
It's all swell until you get bitten.

They do inspire me as they have shown a perfect example of manpower,
The lifting and shifting of those great bricks,
Stacking them together to form a tower,
Scaffolding needed was made from sticks.

The Egyptians inspire me, do they you?

Jake Holmyard (14)
Northolt High School, Northolt

My Inspirational Poem

Inspiration, inspiration,
Oh what does it mean to me?
Is it a bird that flies at night
Or the girl that climbed up the tree?
Inspiration is different in other people's eyes,
Always telling the truth or admitting to lies.
Either way our views will vary
I find things funny, you find them scary.
My inspiration is always random,
Things from a bag to a book,
And a poster and even diamond rings
But the best inspiration in my life has to be my family,
For they are the people that make me, me.

Paige Tyson-Simmons (13)
Northolt High School, Northolt

Sandy

Little Sandy sat in the empty room.
Soon to be lying in her tomb.
She sat shivering, freezing cold.
She picked up her only toy to hold.

She heard the clang of the garden gate.
Her dad home, what would be her fate?
He banged open the front door,
Stormed in her room and put her to the floor.

Kicking and slapping her
He picked her up with her hair
With full force he threw poor innocent Sandy
Down the stairs.

Holly Lane (14)
Northolt High School, Northolt

My Poem

In the future I would like to achieve
Not to betray or to deceive
For this in myself I must believe
From my childish youth I must leave

I don't want to be anyone other than me
To be the greatest lawyer there can be
To protest for all the world to see
I just want to be, to be me.

I'm young and free for the minute
I feel like I'm going to bin it
Things will change and I will spin it
The world will be against me but I will stand strong and I will kill it.

Steven Harding (13)
Northolt High School, Northolt

Poem

They were the key to my goal,
They were the end to my hole,
The person who I most desire,
The one that made me look higher.

I followed in their footsteps,
Because I thought it was for the best.
She was the one I wanted to be,
I wanted to see her in me.

Losing myself
To be someone else
Forgetting my own
For the one I wanted as my clone.

Risha Basit (14)
Northolt High School, Northolt

Inspired

I nspire is nations
N ations reading speeches,
S peeches read to people
P eople that inspire,
I nspire other people who are ready,
R eady to listen endlessly,
E ndlessly about dreams,
D reams that have been inspired.

Martyn Thomas (13)
Northolt High School, Northolt

An Open Window

Walking across the playground I can feel eyes on me
Following me everywhere
Words shoot at me like guns
Guns that never miss their target
Their target is me
I can see my hideout - the toilet door
As I run jeering and insults fill my ears
Finally I push open the worn door
The sound of running taps welcomes me in
Here I am alone
I lock myself in the toilet, flushing away the words
Words that keep piling up
I sit there trying to heal the wounds
Wounds that never stop bleeding
Out of the corner of my eye I see a window
A window letting in light
The window is wide open; laughter creeping out
I can see children that smile up at me
They stretch out their hands ready for me to hold
I am now one of those children, I am truly free.

Bessie Ephgrave (12)
Oxted School, Oxted

Scared

In my dream, I heard a tiger,
So I hid behind a tree.
I was frightened he would eat me up,
'Cause he roared and roared at me.

I woke up scared and sweaty,
Thought I'd sleep with Mum and Del,
But when I went in their room,
Del was snoring really bad.

I climbed between them anyway
With the blanket pulled in tight.
I closed my eyes and wished real hard,
No more tigers, not tonight!

I remembered what Del said,
That your bed is like a book.
If the page on the right is scary,
Turn left and take a look.

I turned to my left and fell asleep.
The tiger wasn't there . . .
But in its place and growling loud
Was a big old grizzly bear!

This time, I woke up shaking!
That really scared me bad!
I had turned both left and right
And they were the only turns I had!

Del was snoring like a buzz saw.
How would I go to sleep?
I'm not too good at counting yet
Or I'd have counted myself some sheep.

I thought about his snores some more, Del sounds just like a bear.
On second thought, a tiger, too, so I got out of there!

Lauren Faulkner (12)
Oxted School, Oxted

I Have A Dream

I have a dream
All animals should be treated with as much respect as we are.

I have a dream
Every person, every animal, every plant has a right to be themselves.

I have a dream
Nobody should be forced into anything that they are unwilling to do.

I have a dream
All are good, but all make mistakes and should learn from these. Though some do not learn, they should still be treated as humans.

I have a dream
Nelson Mandela has the right to free everyone alive from unworthy torture.

I have a dream
There is no need for greed as *I know* that every day, children starve, children walk miles for water, children suffer from disease, children die, because of *our greed*.

So *I have a dream* we should
Think of those in pain.
Then they will have hope and can be believers, believing like true believers.
They will have hope or at least hope to have hope.
They can believe in that hope.
This is what I believe and I believe in you to believe it too.
I believe in you to act now.

Bethany Arnell (12)
Oxted School, Oxted

I Have A Dream

I have a dream
Contradict if you want
I have a dream
That battlefields across the world will be silenced
Of gunshots and of pain
I have a dream, that men will cast aside their lethal weapons
A walk across the destruction, that is of war's making
I have a dream
That dread will release its grip on our hearts
As enemies embrace
I have a dream
That as tears of relief fall to the ground
And hope swells in our minds
That across the world
Weapons will be put to rest
In dark places no one can reach
I have a dream
That death at the hands of another will be no more
That lifeless bodies will not fall to the Earth,
Blood pouring from their throbbing veins
I have a dream
Contradict if you want.

Sophie Conquest (12)
Oxted School, Oxted

Pollution

Pollution, pollution in the air,
Pollution, pollution there's no fresh air,
Pollution, pollution in the ocean,
Pollution, pollution is a disaster potion,
Pollution, pollution better stop,
Before this whole world goes pop!

Luke Thompson (12)
Oxted School, Oxted

I Have A Dream

I have a dream
As many others do
A dream that someday
May be able to come true

It is a dream, of comfort
Love and peace.
A dream that never will be able
To cease

Dreams of others
Are often fantasy
But mine, someday
You will be able to see.

A dream this is for all of us
To share this world
And not make a fuss
What we want is what we need

This dream we want is called World Peace.

Jessica Muscio (12)
Oxted School, Oxted

I Have A Dream

I have a dream.
Do you have a dream?
In my dream there are raindrops on roses and whiskers on kittens.
In my dream the winner would not take it all.
In my dream there would be a super trouper
shining down on every one of us.
In my dream we would all dance through life.
In my dream we would never be on our own.
In my dream we would all be excited about the motion of the ocean
and the sun in the sky each morning.
Now it is time for your dream.

Molly Cook (12)
Oxted School, Oxted

I Have A Dream

My parents want me to study
And read books.
But I have a dream,
A dream to be a singer.
Rock, pop, R&B, any of these will do for me!

With Dad in the car
Music blaring,
Me in the back, just not caring.
I am lost in the rhythm, music and song,
I just can't help but to sing along.

It is not me in the car with Dad,
It's Sophie Potter in concert at Wembley,
Am I really going mad?

Now, for that short time in the car,
I am living my dream,
I am that singer,
Who I've always wanted to be.

Sophie Potter (12)
Oxted School, Oxted

The World Is Like A Human

Stop
Suffocating the world in a thick layer of unbreathable substances!
Stop
Feeding the Earth and start feeding the bins with your litter.
Stop
Destroying the oceans which are the life blood of the world!

The world can be thought of like a human.
This human is asthmatic and limping along;
Help it recover from its injuries and staunch its wounds;
Start
Giving it an inhaler and a crutch to help it on its way!

Genevieve Hadida
Oxted School, Oxted

I Have A Dream

I have a dream that the sun will shine again.
I have a dream that there will be peace on Earth.
I have a dream that humanity is caring.
I have a dream that poverty is abolished.
I have a dream that I can do something for the world.
I have a dream that one finger can change it forever.
I had a dream that I was there.

I had a nightmare and I saw reality!
I had a nightmare and I saw the painful wars.
I had a nightmare and I saw Mother Nature dying.
I had a nightmare and I saw the old sick people.
I had a nightmare and I saw the people on the streets.
I had a nightmare and I saw the ozone layer as I looked down from above.
I had a nightmare and I saw the children dying.
I had a nightmare and I saw the supreme poverty.
From then I knew we weren't trying hard enough.
So do your best, let's fight all this together.

Dylan Middleton (11)
Oxted School, Oxted

They Will

They will put out the fire
They will save your life
They will arrest the man
Who stabbed you with a knife
They will heal the wound
That goes deep into your chest
They will put you in the bed
Where you will sleep and rest
But now is when you realise
The emergency services are the best!

Tom Thornley (13)
Oxted School, Oxted

War

War
Is going on everywhere
War
Leaders trying to stop it
War
Emergency services helping people
War
Nothing stops the enemy killing
War
Comes and goes in leaps and bounds
War
Leaves buildings damaged
War
Is happening all over the world
Please stop war now!

Eleanor Harber
Oxted School, Oxted

Emergency Services

They're out all day,
Just work, no play,
Risking their lives,
And giving each other high fives,
They work day and night,
The fires they fight,
The criminals they arrest,
The people they test,
All to make sure,
We follow the law!

Sam Carpenter (13)
Oxted School, Oxted

The Drunk Man

The shame you felt,
When he walked out your front door.
Coming home drunk,
With anger in his eyes,
And shouting, waking the kids,
Who were sound asleep upstairs.

The doorbell rings, knocking,
Bang, bang, bang,
Trying to get in.
He's been at it again;
Causing chaos in the streets at night.

When will he ever stop?
The kids are worried,
It's not fair,
For them to see the man,
Who acts violently to their mum.

Something has to be done,
The kids don't deserve this.
Why should they?

Their father is no longer himself,
He's drunk and violent.
He may hurt the kids,
If it gets out of hand.

It's midnight and he's upstairs,
She has no choice but to dial 999.
Quietly they knock on the door,
Creep upstairs,
And take the no longer father,
But drunk man away,
So no one gets hurt.

Emma Felton (13)
Selsdon High School, Croydon

Untitled

The sun was ice,
The moon was fire,
The sky was Hell,
The Earth was Heaven,
And I was empty.
I had nothing left,
But to end my life . . .
To end it now.
But someone was there,
In the bright light.
When I saw His face,
I couldn't speak,
I fell in front of Him,
Looking for a way
To thank Him,
Because He changed my life
Immediately!
Now I had a heart
A heart full with love and happiness,
Because of Him . . .
. . . God!

Magdalina Strumelieva (13)
Selsdon High School, Croydon

He Had A Dream . . .

He had a dream that one day,
Little black boys and little black girls would play around with each other.
He had a dream that one day,
Black people would be treated as equally as white people.
He had a dream that one day,
Little black boys and little black girls would be brother and sister to white boys and girls.
He had a dream that one day,
Black people could drink out of the same water fountain as white people.
He had a dream that one day,
There would be no racism.
He had a dream that one day,
Black people wouldn't have to give up their seats for white people on the bus.
He had a dream that one day,
Black people wouldn't have to pay more money for the bus than white people.
That person who had that dream was Martin Luther King,
And his dream came true.
He had a dream . . .

Imanna Kirby (13)
Selsdon High School, Croydon

Untitled

I'm having difficulty
I can't find any ideas
For a poem I have to write

I just sit here staring
At a blank piece of paper
And a pen full of ink

I look at the birds
Flying through the sky
I look at the fish
Swimming in the pond

I listen to music
From pop to rap
I watch the TV
For a good hour or so

Inspiration, inspiration,
It just comes too slow
Hey, wait a minute
I think I know . . .

Courtney Bain (14)
Selsdon High School, Croydon

Dreams

His dream was to be heard,
His voice lost in the crowd,
Deep in his veins somewhere
There was change.

He no longer had anger,
Just words stronger than strength.
He had completed every black man's dream
Of making history, of making a change,
Having a purpose in life.

His dream was to make a change;
His dream was to inspire people;
His dream was to make a difference;
His dream was to be noticed;
His dream was to make history;
His dream was to be the president of America.

He finally had accomplished all his dreams,
What if he didn't try to fulfil his dreams?
Where would he be now?

Paul Dawkins (12)
Selsdon High School, Croydon

Evacuation

I'm so nervous,
I don't feel strong
A tug at my mum
As the train comes along

I don't know anyone
It's really not fair
I'm closing my eyes
As I speak a little prayer

The children are crying
They are not having fun
I just want to go home
But nothing can be done.

The train pulls over
I'm here for many days
But I'm still always hoping
That maybe I'll run away.

Nathasha Berry (13)
Selsdon High School, Croydon

Not Just Yourself . . .

Think about other people in this world . . .
All the people who suffer from hunger,
All the people who are always in danger,
Think about the people who fought for us in wars,
All the people who lost their loved ones,
All the people who got murdered in the past,
All the people who are homeless,
Think about the people who have changed this world,
All the people who love and care about you,
All the people who suffer from disabilities,
Just think of all these people . . .
Not just yourself!

Clay Pel-Is (13)
Selsdon High School, Croydon

Dreams At Young Ages

My dream is to become a role model for
All those people who enjoy what I do.

My dream is to design clothes for all those
Shopaholics.

My dream is to be a doctor and treat
All the sick people who can't get and afford
Good medical help.

My dream is to go back to my home countries
And see my family and friends.

My dream is to become a great footballer and
Play for my home city.

My dream is to become a famous actor for
All those film lovers.

My dream is to fill out my destiny.

Cindy Okech (13)
Selsdon High School, Croydon

I Have A Wish!

I have a wish that there is no violence

I have a wish that at night I can have a sleep
Without being woken by police sirens

I have a wish that gangs can go to different
Ends without getting stabbed.

I have a wish that families can grow
Up forgetting the struggle
They had at youth

I have a wish that we can drive
Cars and get on public transport without
Worrying about the pollution.

Reece Wright (11)
Selsdon High School, Croydon

Emptiness

Imagine a world in silence
Imagine a world without strength
Imagine a world without violence
Imagine a world without cities
Imagine a world without people
Imagine people without care
Imagine a world without love
Imagine a world without a soul
Imagine a life without a family
Imagine a world in emptiness
Imagine a heart without a beat
Imagine one in our lifetime
Imagine chocolate without a taste
Imagine a kiss without meaning
Imagine everything is emptiness.

Sadia Kubie (13)
Selsdon High School, Croydon

I Have A Dream

I have a dream that one day
I will become whatever I want,
And have a successful life with my wife.

I have a dream that one day
My children's children will live a great life
And work for the society.

I have a dream that one day
I will help the poor and the blind.

I have a dream that before I die,
The world will be a better place.
The streets will be peaceful
And the houses will be quieter.

I have a dream.

Abel Kinganga (14)
Selsdon High School, Croydon

World Without War

A world without war would be a peaceful place
Knowing that you can walk down the street,
All the time feeling safe,
With no rubble falling to your feet,
Knowing your loved ones are alive,
Not in trenches dug down low,
With a cold gun pressed against their side.
Fighting with those too young to go.
Knowing you're safe in your bed.
When all is silent in the night,
Without the sound of bombs up ahead,
And not allowed to turn on the light.
World without war would be so great.
So making changes in the world be your fate.

Tarnya Grover (14)
Selsdon High School, Croydon

I Have A Dream!

I go to sleep every night
Thinking
Thinking of people suffering and dying
I see all these boys rolling with knives
But they don't know
They are taking someone's precious life

I want to make the world a better place
Stop fighting over a colour of race!
I've got to stop it
Now!
But I don't know how!

Edgar Morais (13)
Selsdon High School, Croydon

I Am . . .

I am the white chocolate my sister eats,
I am my mum who pushes me to achieve,
And my dad who works for what he has.
I am my laptop that connects me to the world,
I am the birds and the trees,
I am the kiss that touches your smooth cheeks.
I am the shoes and clothes,
I am my friends that brighten my day.
I am every happy moment,
I am a brilliant person,
Because of you.

Yasmin Allwood (14)
Selsdon High School, Croydon

Four Of A Kind

I have sad friends,
Bad friends,
Mad friends.

Friends who smile,
Friends who scowl,
Friends who scream,
And friends who howl.

Friends of every shape and size,
Friends who tell the truth and friends who lie.

But none of my friends,
See themselves as they are,
And that's beautiful, funny,
Exciting and smart.

And even if it takes,
Every thought in my mind,
I will make them believe,
That they are *four of a kind.*

Holly McCarthy (14)
The Cottesloe School, Leighton Buzzard

Message

Actions can hurt,
They can create wounds but they will heal,
But words last a lifetime and sometimes beyond.
They can remain and be remembered,
Make a ripple in time,
Engraved and embedded in brains,
And inspire other minds.

I wish I could speak out,
And have my words written in the history books.
But I am one voice.
Yes, others have achieved what seems to be the impossible:
Martin Luther King, Winston Churchchill and Lesley Choyce.
It can be done,
But it is by no means an easy task.

All of us have a message which we wish to speak out,
But the opportunities to be heard are not always so easy to come by.
We have to carry our desires and wishes every day,
The impossible ambition contained in a normal life,
Cocooned and imprisoned,
With the feeling of never breaking free.

'Every day, we are told there are people worse off than ourselves;
The poor, living and struggling with poverty,
People who have experienced a natural disaster and need help,
Victims from conflict,
And others who are not able-bodied.
Even though we are reminded of them,
We push them to the back of our minds,
And forget that they exist.
But yet these people need our help.
We are lucky to be born where we are,
These people did not ask for their life,
And it should be our responsibility to help them,
So please, help to make the world a better place.

Help and donate to those without.
Help and volunteer and meet so many new people.
Help and change your views and help your conscience.
Help to make a better tomorrow for the next generations.'

That is the message on my shoulders.

Adreen Hart-Rule (17)
The Cottesloe School, Leighton Buzzard

Warfare Poem - The Causes Of War

The disgusting thing that is war
Starts off with money.
Greedy, selfish leaders
Think that war is funny.

They think it is as fun as playing Risk,
The tactical war board game.
They say, 'It is for the good of our people.'
What they mean is they are filled with blame.

They blame other countries
For things they didn't do,
Just to start a war.
They say, 'It was you!'

They like blood and gore,
And enjoy chopping heads off.
This only causes them to suffer,
As their plan will backfire and cough.

Just like World War II,
When the UK hit the Germans hard.
Lots of people died
And left lots of people scarred.

This also caused homelessness,
Orphaned children and the poor.
War is a terrible thing
And these are the causes of war.

Will Guyon (14)
The Cottesloe School, Leighton Buzzard

One

It only takes one action,
One word,
One person,
One group,
To change the world.

It only takes one woman,
One woman called Joan of Arc,
To join up dressed as a man,
To give women equal rights.

It only takes one woman,
One woman called Rosa Parks,
To say, 'No I won't!'
To give the outcasts a chance.

It only takes one man,
One man called Winston Churchill,
To Britain that we shall never surrender,
To give England a fighting chance.

It only takes one man,
One man called Martin Luther King,
To say, 'I have a dream'
To change the path of the future.

It only takes one group,
One group called the 'Suffrage',
To say we want to vote,
To give women a political chance.

It only takes one action,
One word,
One person,
One group,
To change the world.

Scarlett Miles (13)
The Cottesloe School, Leighton Buzzard

I Have A Dream

I have a dream,
An ambition I aim to fulfil,
To save millions of lives,
I will make people see
I will change their selfish,
Uncaring minds.

Have you see the starvation,
The pure desperation
Of youngsters whose biggest wish
Is just to survive?
Have you seen
The helpless pain they have to endure?

It sickens me to think,
As you're tucking into your meal,
A baby will die,
An innocent human,
Who has all the same rights as you,
Will have their life taken from them.

It takes the heartless,
To ignore this cry for help.
A plead for just a minute's input,
A little donation that can go so far,
A little consideration that can save a child's life,
Just think twice.

Who's to say,
It should be you next?
You sat with nothing but hope,
Just waiting to fade away
Slowly and painfully.
I have a dream.

Yasmin Chambers (14)
The Cottesloe School, Leighton Buzzard

Homeless

Wide eyes staring,
From white faces, dingy places,
Soaring buildings,
Grubby clothes, names nobody knows.

Sleeping bags rolled,
Newspaper sheets on cold streets,
Little pots labelled,
Change Please,
No one sees.

Why are they here?
From nice homes; why do they roam?
Young children,
Lost in the city, full of sorrow and pity.

How can we help?
Needing hugs, needing drugs?
Give them money?
No, give them food, change their mood.

Give them shelter,
Give them heat, lots to eat,
Talk to them;
What went wrong? Away too long.

We all need help,
Life isn't easy, leaves you feeling queasy,
People on the streets,
Need care, if you dare.

Make a change,
Write a letter, make it better,
Everyone needs to work as a team,
Look after each other, look after your brother.

Harry McCartney (13)
The Cottesloe School, Leighton Buzzard

Words Of The World

Lives were changed,
Differences were made,
Hearts were broken,
Words were spoken.

'We will fight,' said he,
He believed,
That we would win,
Our right to fight for freedom.

'One small step for man,' said he,
He believed,
That we would learn,
And see what we yearned to see.

'The lady is not for turning,' said she,
She believed,
To change her country
And people, would believe in better.

'Votes for women,' said she,
She believed,
That equality was here
And women should fight for their right.

Words were said and words were read.
People believed and people deceived.
People died and people cried.

Think of what they did, a second to recall,
To think of those who helped us all.

Words are just words,
But when spoken with truth and belief,
They are magic.

Heather Potton (13)
The Cottesloe School, Leighton Buzzard

How Can It Be?

How can it be,
A man,
Who can't even do his job well,
Gets billions of pounds for doing nothing
And another man gets nothing,
For doing his job well?

How can there be,
Such a difference in the world,
That someone has more money
Than they know what to do with
And someone else
Can't even feed their own family?

How can it be,
On one side of the world,
People are dying and suffering form preventable diseases
And on the other,
People are paying thousands of pounds
Just to change the way they look?

How can it be,
That only one in five African children go to school
And other parents are paying thousands
To send their children to school?

How can it be,
That we're all cosy in our central-heated houses
Whilst the homeless prepare
For another night on the dirty streets?

There is no justice. It is not fair.
But what are *you* going to do about it?

Eddie Wiggins (14)
The Cottesloe School, Leighton Buzzard

Words

Words . . . Just words,
But words . . . Can make the world of difference
And words can change the world.

'I have a dream'
Martin Luther King,
He made a difference,
Worked as a team.

'Never surrender'
Winston Churchill,
He made a difference,
Was prepared to kill.

'No I won't!'
Rosa Parks,
She made a difference,
She made her mark.

'Yes we can'
Barack Obama,
He made a difference
Won votes of fans.

All these people
Just used words . . .
To succeed in what they
Wanted to accomplish!

Words . . . Can mean the world,
Words . . . Can make the world of difference,
Words . . . Can change the world!

Alice Berry (14)
The Cottesloe School, Leighton Buzzard

Why?

Words can change the world.
One thing you say,
'Why?'
Can make the world of difference.

Martin Luther King asked,
'Why
Are white people better than black people?'
Look where we are now.

Winston Church asked,
'Why
Should the Jews be killed?'
Look where we are now.

Gandhi asked,
'Why
Should we solve our battles with violence?'
Look where we are now.

Neil Armstrong asked,
'Why
Can't Man explore the moon?'
Look where we are now.

So, words can change the world
And questions can change your life.
So say what you think and feel,
And see for yourself what they can do.

Shannan Mitchener (14)
The Cottesloe School, Leighton Buzzard

Bullying

Bullying can destroy lives,
Most bullies are proud of it,
Bullies these days use knives,
No way to get out of it,
Now you're feeling so depressed,
Doing things you don't want to do,
Now you're forced not to rest,
Just because they want you to.

You're soon feeling so small,
Someone should do something,
You used to always have it all,
Now you've got nothing,
You're soon facing paranoia,
You wish that you were someone else,
Now they've got punishment for ya,
You're seen shouting for help.

You're thinking about suicide,
You've been pushed to the edge,
You look over and die inside,
It's a sheer drop off the ledge,
Once you've been pushed this far,
You just can't stop yourself,
You go home, it feels so far,
You hang yourself by your belt.

Alfie Gardner-Potter (13)
The Cottesloe School, Leighton Buzzard

Future Of War

An explosion here,
An explosion there,
They don't spend,
A second to care.

One life gone,
Another about to go,
Help us now
Or let them go.

Eat that apple,
Drink that water,
Just spare some time,
For those starving children.

Time has come,
Time to change,
To change our world,
To change people around us.

Poverty to become history,
Wars to be totally wiped out.
The past to be forgotten
And the future starts now.

George Langston (14)
The Cottesloe School, Leighton Buzzard

I Have A Dream

Welcome to my world
It's drowning in malicious people
I have a dream
To make all more endurable.

Welcome to this world
People trust in drugs
I have a dream
For drugs to become forbidden.

Welcome to my world
People hurt others for no outstanding reason
I have a dream
Where people heal, not cause pain.

Welcome to this world
People are not treated equally
I have a dream
That people understand differences.

Welcome to this bad, bad world
I have a dream
That goodness, happiness and love will rule.

Beth Styles (14)
The Cottesloe School, Leighton Buzzard

Men Of The Past

May every step be brighter than the last
Due to the actions performed by the people of the past
They gave it their all for a brighter today
So black people have their own say.

Those great men let their actions not be forgotten
Their words shall be carried by the sons they've begotten
Future generations shall bellow their speech
In the words that they actively preach.

Rodney Peters (14)
The Cottesloe School, Leighton Buzzard

Inspiration Of The World

Joan of Arc, God told me
Make your mark, God told me
Fight for more, God told me
Go to war, God told me
Never surrender, God told me.

Rosa Parks, I'm staying here
Make our marks, I'm staying here
You know how, I'm staying here
Get out of the way, I'm staying here.

Winston Churchill, I believe
To protect our will, I believe
Save the kingdom, I believe
To trust our soldiers, I believe.

Barack Obama, yes we can
In our armour, yes we can
Fight for Man, yes we can
This is my plan, yes we can
Live for America, yes we can.

Sammie Joanne Wootten (14)
The Cottesloe School, Leighton Buzzard

A World Without Racism!

A world without racism
What kind of world would that be?
No oppression or judging of colour of skin
Just judging by the content of character
All people equal and free

All boys and girls black and white
All who are God's creations
Together shall all join hands in harmony
Brothers and sisters, all who are mixed race
Together in peace not war

No person shall walk alone
No mountain will be too high
No differences between human beings
Should get in the way of becoming one
The world in immunity

A world without racism
A better place to be.

Zara Ashton (13)
The Cottesloe School, Leighton Buzzard

War On War

I have a dream
That one day war will not be a word,
That one day guns will drop,
That one day bullets will not pop,

I have a dream
That one day there will be peace,
That one day war will have no cost,
That one day no more lives will be lost,

I have a dream
That one day the war with war will be won.

Chris Worlock (13)
The Cottesloe School, Leighton Buzzard

Poverty

This is where we fight
to stop world hunger,
to stop world suffering.
When every person can go to sleep on a full stomach
And not dread the long morning walk to fetch the water.

We must fight
To provide medicine for the poor hospitals
With diseased children waiting to die
And to provide running water from taps
When one day the dry droughts end
And crops will finally grow on moist soil.

We must fight
To find shelter from rain and storms
With a real bed, not just a hard mud floor.
To give all newborn babies around the world
The jabs and injections they need.
There must be ways of stopping all the bad in the world.

Emma Whittome (14)
The Cottesloe School, Leighton Buzzard

War

Gunfire and explosions surround you
The constant ringing and knowing of death
If you make one wrong move
It's over.

Your friends dying all around
Not knowing when you will see your family again
Unsure when you will get your next meal.

Darkness is surrounding you
Sewer water swimming with rats
Noise so deafening your ears bleed
So scared . . . waiting to go home.

Tom Herbert (14)
The Cottesloe School, Leighton Buzzard

Above All Others

A country that needs healing
above all others,
A country that needs guidance
above all others,
A country that needs a helping hand
above all others.
A country in a war
to end all others.

But not quite so.

This country should be whole
The help should have been offered
The war should be over

And it will be over

President Obama

Hope.

Chloe Brown (14)
The Cottesloe School, Leighton Buzzard

Segregation

Why was there segregation
between black and white?
There is no reason
I can think of, all it is
is a colour like
red or green or blue.

Segregation was everywhere
you looked, buses, benches
trains and more,
black and white are both equal
so why did it carry on
for so long?

Ben Cleaver (13)
The Cottesloe School, Leighton Buzzard

Untitled

I've always said life is like a box of chocolates, you never know which one you're going to get,
And I still live by that philosophy, and my only son Forrest I'll never regret.
Some say he's slow, dumb and docile, he's a few slices short of a loaf,
Whilst some go so low to call him as stupid and dumb as an oaf.

I've always been one to shower him with praise, love and affection,
My heart weeps as he asks me what such simple words mean,
a sign of his simple reflection.
Had to sell my body to the head of a local state school in order to get him a place,
And even though his IQ is only seventy-five, it gave me such joy when he realised. His happy face.

He'd always been different, instead of braces on teeth they were on his limbs,
And of course, it gave the locals further reinforcement that he was just completely dim.
Although he tried his best at school he found his talent for running,
And even gained a scholarship and place on the local football team despite continued shunning.

A mother's joy, I felt exactly that when I found out he enrolled at the University of Alabama,
He made me so proud, the way he dealt with all the insults, the jibes and punched them down as if with a hammer.
So it came to a shock when I realised he wanted to go in the army after leaving university,
But what could I argue? He said he fitted into the army like a round peg and liked the diversity.

My anxiety was bittersweet, every day I worried about him dying but knew he loved serving his nation.
A few years passed, and learned he was safe, unharmed and only with a wound in the buttocks as a sign of compensation.
Told me all about his adventures, his Bubba, his shrimps and his ping pong fascination,
He was quickly noticed, twenty-five thousand dollars offered a solution to money complications.

Then he was off with the wind again, my Forrest, striving, searching,

screaming for his Jenny,
I felt the strong similarity to The American Dream and Steinbeck's Lenny.
They may view him to be a mouse, but to me he'll always be a man,
The one who stumbles across so much but never really seems to give a damn.

So I sit here in my bedroom with a brilliant view over Greenbow,
And that is when it first rushed over me, a feeling my heart was getting slow.
Death is inevitable, I know that much and I've passed my prime,
I think about Forrest and a solitary tear falls down my cheek, I guess it is just my time.
From the money he's made I get my maid to get in contact with him wherever he may be,
It will be just like old times, when we fished together by the lake resembling a sea.

For one final time I see him rush in with that same old look of curiosity on his face,
And I tell him I love him and tell him to be strong as I finally give up the chase.
This was just my story and that will never change and will always stay as it seems,
This was just my take reflecting my wants for Forrest, penned in all my hopes and dreams.

James Reynolds (17)
The Douay Martyrs School, Ickenham

I Have A Dream

Passing through a time of trouble and darkness
I look for a time of hope and brightness
Looking through a time of sorrow and bloodshed
I can see a time of unity.

What I hope for is
What I believe in
And what I believe in
Is my hope.

Ashik Santimon (15)
The Douay Martyrs School, Ickenham

An Excerpt From A Dream . . . Or A Nightmare?

Dreams are wonderful, magical, enchanting things
A place where you can go and become your own king
Bunnies and turtles and penguins in suits
Riches and treasure and diamond encrusted boots!
Dreams can be fun, until the morning sun
That's when they end, until you go to bed
And dream through the night and rest your soft head
But dreams can turn for the worse
Like an old witch's curse
They can make you scream at night
And give you a horrible fright
You will toss and turn,
Your head will burn
But you can't escape
This must be fate
Can you ever wake
Or is this just fake?
You're so tired . . .
From these nightmares,
These dreams get you fired
No one seems to care . . .
Face down in the dirt
You say, 'It doesn't hurt.'
You've finally had enough!
It's time to get tough
You're a prisoner in this cage
You work for no wage
You get pushed and shoved
Yet still, you're not loved
What they say is true
There's nothing you can do
This is something you must accept
You are . . . truly inept
Stepped on like a mat
Even by homeless cats
Spiralling down

You've lost your gold crown
But you keep your chin up
Don't worry; you can regain your crown
Turn your life upside down
Start all over again
Begin anew.

Mark Migallos (14)
The Douay Martyrs School, Ickenham

Death Of A Dream

He had a dream
His words were weapons
When unleashed, they cut deep and sank into his opponents
Did his people ever know freedom until now?

They responded!
They decided they'd flex their weapons too . . .
Only, theirs was a gun.

When the trigger was pulled,
Time itself stopped
For the welcoming of death.

His presence was felt,
People stared.
He shouted.

The shooter stood, gazing.
The bullet manoeuvred in and out
Of the red heat haze.

The heavy particles clogged the air
Delaying the bullet a few tiny milliseconds.

The bullet hit . . .

Blood splattered.
He dropped with a thud
Under a Memphis Sky.
Life was lost.

Andy Luu (15)
The Douay Martyrs School, Ickenham

The Little Mermaid

Way beneath the deep blue sea
Wished a mermaid princess who thought that she
Didn't quite belong to her world
She'd rather run like a human girl
She wished that she could drink a potion and turn to human
But she knew her father would be fumin'

One day she sat on a rock
But as the sunset came she got a shock
In the sea her prince was about to drown
And on the mermaid's face appeared a frown
She could not allow this prince to die
So if she could save him she would definitely try

In the end she saved the man
Then back to the sea she swam
But the time she had spent with the prince
She had remembered ever since
She tried to find someone to help
She even asked a piece of kelp

Then one day she turned to a witch
Who had a rather evil twitch
The witch kindly gave her human legs
But in return she didn't want fish eggs
The witch asked for the mermaid's voice
The mermaid agreed and simply rejoiced

The girl woke up on the shore
But on her, there was a new item she'd never worn
A pair of fantastic human legs
She found the prince and to stay with him she begged
The prince kindly said that she could stay
And eventually love braved hooray, hooray

The sea witch did not like what she saw
So she tricked the prince and he swore
To marry this mysterious woman
But the mermaid found out and she was stubborn
So she decided to put an end to this
Then she and the witch fought for the prince's kiss

Eventually the mermaid won the fight
And the handsome prince seized his knife
He killed the witch and broke the spell
That kept the mermaid's voice in a shell
The dead witch now lies beneath the water
And the mermaid and the prince lived happily ever after.

Katherine Hourihan (13)
The Douay Martyrs School, Ickenham

I Have A Dream

I have a dream
That time could hold still for me.
If only for this moment
As my soul surrenders
To my heart's resolve

When what lies inside
Is worn on my sleeve
So delicately balancing
On the edge of forever.
While dark skies are beckoning
And the prospect of night
Shines brighter than the sun.

With Heaven's rains now caressing us
So clearly painted scenes
From my watercolour memory
Of what has been
And of what will be
To be loved
As no soul has known
When hope allows destiny
To give life to love
And sets it free
I have a dream
That time could hold still for me.

Kirsty Brown (16)
The Douay Martyrs School, Ickenham

I Have A Dream

'I have a dream that one day, the sons of former slaves and the sons of former slave owners will be able to sit down together on the table of brotherhood'.

The famous words of Martin Luther King,
Believe in yourself and it shall bring,
The amazing dreams you wish to aspire,
Do not hold back, continue to aim higher.

Leave yesterday's troubles in the past,
And look forward to the future,
If they want to hold you back they can be last,
And you can be their teacher.

God will guide you,
But your determination will see you through,
Just continue to believe,
And imagine what you can achieve.

For you, Barack Obama,
Have given young black youths the key,
And released them from their trauma,
Which can now set them free.

You have given us the strength,
And given us the faith,
You have increased the length,
And tightened the lace,

Which makes us run faster,
And helps us move past the,
Betrayal and violence,
So no one suffers in silence.

For you have made black history,
About what it is meant to be,
Not torture and misery,
But happiness and destiny.

Sherree Rosario (16)
The Douay Martyrs School, Ickenham

A Dream Is Your Place

A dream is your place,
Your very own sanctuary,
You stare it in the face,
And you know it's where you want to be.
Nowhere on this Earth,
Can be as special as this,
Where I am right now,
Is the ultimate definition of bliss.

No never! You can't make me leave my place,
It's my only escape,
Oh no I'm having that dream again,
The life-altering moment is starting to take shape.
The monster from my nightmares,
He managed to break out,
Please save me, save me,
In my place nobody can hear my shout.

Trying to smash through the portal,
I'm frightened, I'm scared.
I wasn't made immortal,
There I was crawling my way through,
The dark shadows which consumed me,
Desperately trying to look to,
The one place which can set me free.

Finally I'm back,
In the safety of my room,
Reality is your true fate,
Escaping it you just can't do,
I sit up erect in my bed,
So many thoughts are swirling in my head,
So gently I mutter to myself making it easier, so it seemed,
It's okay, just relax,
I had a dream, I had a dream.

Sasha Garrett (14)
The Douay Martyrs School, Ickenham

My Yellow Brick Road

I have a dream, a dream which one day will come true,
A dream that's not too big but not too small,
A dream that I wish to accomplish.

I want to travel the world, do and see amazing things,
I want to get a good job and be very successful, but to do all that,
I need to get my head down in school.

I want to settle down and find a man that truly loves me,
I want to have a massive wedding and a big family,
I want to die with the people I love and cherish around me,
I want to die a very old woman,
I want to die knowing I've had a good life.

I want to do what I want to do,
I want to make mistakes and learn from them,
I don't want any regrets,
I don't want things holding me back,
I want to say yes to everything that is possible.

I love the friends I have at the moment and I don't want to lose them now.
They are absolutely incredible! I can be myself around them.
We can laugh, joke and not have a care in the world about what other people think about us.
So, good luck finding your best friends because I've already got all the best ones.

My family are mad, but I love them to pieces.
They've made me who I am today because I'm so loved.
I'm so grateful for it because I love being me.
If I didn't have my family, only God knows what I'd do.

I have got everything I need at the moment.
No, my life isn't perfect, but nothing is perfect!
I'm only young and I have years ahead of me.
I can't wait to see where life takes me, the future is unpredictable.

Charlotte Mitchell (13)
The Douay Martyrs School, Ickenham

Policeman

One day when I was walking
With my friend, Sam
Me listening, him talking
Then I saw the great man.

He wore a coat and long hat
Big boots with a black strap
A big belt with a wooden bat
Whilst trying to save a cat.

The suspect ran
He chased
He was stopped by a pan
Then there was laughter

When I went up to him
With his partner Tim
While he put some rubbish in the bin
He pointed to his hair and said, 'I need a trim'

When he was alone
He took me to the station
All I could hear was a drone
Then he said to come to the secret location

After college
With lots of friends
Now with lots of knowledge
And a community to mend

I did all the training
Without complaining
Every youngster we're blaming
This is the work of a
Policeman.

Joseph McDonnell (13)
The Douay Martyrs School, Ickenham

A Poem For The Nihilistic Generation

They don't dream or aspire to be,
Anything more than expected,
Limits and boundaries mould plasticine,
And originality is corrected.

Pitiless time devours the years;
Don't be left hollow, full of bitter regret,
For a life lived in vain is never sincere,
And a life cruel time will shortly forget.

We don't dream and fail to see,
Where to place our hearts,
Us 'middle children of history',
Half-try and fail to make our mark.

Though I was never one to make an excuse,
For lack of ambition or drive,
The invented glass ceilings above us, we use,
To spare us from failure, to hide.

But you *must* dream and strive to acquire,
Glory and success,
Quench your deepest heart's desires,
And leave a story when you rest.

Who will flourish in life, with a zesty ardour?
There's not a moment to waste!
Thriving on new passion, we're hungrily reborn,
We finally begin life, we *finally* have a taste.

I *will* dream and I *will* see,
I *will* go far and live,
In this world I *will* succeed.
Who's with me?

Sean Donnelly (16)
The Douay Martyrs School, Ickenham

I Have A Dream

I look around me
And all I see is . . . is
Is the same old me.

I have dreams, I have hopes,
Just hard to let them out.
I need to be free
To become someone
In the life I have.

I am making a choice
Choices which will have consequences
I will learn from mistakes
Mistakes which will make me a better person,
A better daughter and a better friend.

When I grow up
I want my sister, to look up to me
To think
That's who I want to be.

Go to university
Make new friends
A new beginning
Till life's end.

When my last day of learning comes
I will scream and shout
To have fulfilled my ambitions
The thing that will always follow me is:
I'm proud of me
I'm proud of my dreams.

Natalie Potts (13)
The Douay Martyrs School, Ickenham

The Dream Of A Perfect World . . .

The dream . . . I have a dream . . .
That the sky of the world will be clear blue,
And the western wind calmly whistling,
And the great dove freedom flew,
And lush green grass slowly growing.

I have a dream . . .
That the polar bear will live,
And the poverty gone,
And the rich man will give,
And the war be none.

I have a dream . . .
That the world is rebuilt,
And every creature kept with care,
And every child free from guilt,
And every soul treated fair.

I have a dream . . .
That the forest will grow,
And every desert will stay,
And every Arctic place will snow,
And every coral won't go grey.

I have a dream . . .
Sons and daughters of Adam and Eve,
Will never ever need to grieve,
And that our only world,
Will look like one precious big pearl . . .

This dream can come true . . .
But only by you . . .

Naeem Dowlut (14)
The Douay Martyrs School, Ickenham

The Game

One day when I was playing that game,
The gameplay was good
But the graphics were lame,
The guy behind it must be ashamed
Everything was poor and he was to be blamed.
I think I could do better
Anyone could,
This was as fun as cutting wood.

Then there's the other game
The best thing ever made,
It was so addictive
It was the only thing I played.
When I played online I had a blast
Too bad I always came last!

It all comes down to the fact they are fun,
Churning out millions
The deal is done,
But without these games where would we be?
Dull lifeless beings with nothing to do or see.
Now that the poem has come to a close
It's time to get back to that game
Be warned though,
Once you try it you'll never be the same!

Arjan Singh Lall (13)
The Douay Martyrs School, Ickenham

I Have A Dream

Do you have a dream?
Dreams can become a reality,
If you just believe.

You could dream of being a race car driver,
Or even a diver.
When you're a race car driver you'll be like a cheetah,
When you're a diver you'll be among Olympic stars
And dine in five star hotels for a fiver.

If you want to be an actress
You will be Kate Winslet at the Oscars,
Winning your award,
People chanting your name,
You will have loads of fame.

If you want to be a model,
Strut your stuff and you'll see,
You will be like Kate Moss
And own your own clothing line,
Then you will shine,
Like a star in the deep blue sky.

So, now you can see that anyone's dream can come true,
If you just believe in yourself and your dream will come to you.

Helen Jones (13)
The Douay Martyrs School, Ickenham

?

We should dream of a world
Where people don't abstain from complaint,
They make their voices heard
Instead of keeping so quiet and faint,
A world where it's cool to be a nerd,
Where nations are filled to the brim with individuals,
And there are no more people wanting to be a part of the herd,
A world where we have no unnecessary vigils.
But a dream is a natural phenomena of the mind,
They only become reality when we enlist a goal and a purpose,
A target beyond the call of duty where your requirements are surplus,
Our world has been developed by the visions of a few,
Now the lands of many have adopted these traditions,
But we are still confronted by a globe of people
With this nervous disposition
A condition where the repetition of fear is still in their heads,
They are intimidated by the weak and
Upheld by the strong,
But this balance of power is unknown and leads to so much wrong,
The people weak of mind need educating.
Wake up.

Jack Haynes (16)
The Douay Martyrs School, Ickenham

The Three Of Us

There are three of us,
Myself, Failure and Purpose.
It's hard being with those two,
Failure is my doom but also at my doorstep,
And Purpose is on no one's side,
He could let Failure bully me,
He could help promote me,
The three of us walk alongside each other,
I dare not look at them,
They are big.
All I want is to succeed,
But not so high that when Failure attacks me,
I fall an inch and not a mile.
It goes on forever and ever,
The wondering whose turn it is next,
Why don't I ever get a turn?
But before I forget to take a breath,
I do recall the sensation of fluttering eyelids.
Time to stop my nonsense and take what is coming.
Failure and Purpose will always stick around,
Even in the back of my mind.

Samantha Chigbo (14)
The Douay Martyrs School, Ickenham

Dreams

I'm in a dream,
Filled with screams,
How can I escape from here?
Oh I am so surrounded by fear.

I have no dream, no purpose, no goal,
I feel as if I'm wandering through a black hole.
How can I escape from here?
Oh I am so surrounded by fear.

Anna Alvarez (14)
The Douay Martyrs School, Ickenham

I Have A Dream

I have a dream . . .
I want to travel,
Travel the whole wide world,
Making it better,
A better place for everyone.

I have a dream . . .
I want to feed the hungry,
And make everyone happy,
And bless all the poor souls
That are less fortunate than me.

I have a dream,
That can become reality
Nobody can stop me,
Nothing is in my path,
No human being is better than the next.

I have a dream,
That I can change the world.
I have a dream,
That can and will become true.

Alice Connolly (12)
The Douay Martyrs School, Ickenham

Summer

It's the warm breeze on your face,
The sun lighting your hair.
The sound of flip-flops on the ground,
Reminds me that summer is here.
The taste of cool ice cream in your mouth,
The sound of birds whistling in the air.
The waves mixing against the horizon,
It's my favourite time of the year!

Tara Swann (14)
The Douay Martyrs School, Ickenham

The Chasm

A glimmer of hope exists
Like light flickering through the cold bars of a cage
A glimmer of hope
To beat the suffering clothed in the cloak of misery

The light is infectious
It spreads through the hearts of children
Who dream
In delight

Of their next day's only meal
Of going to school
Of being safe
And warm . . .
In their deceased mother's loving arms.

The children of the first world dream of trivial things
Blissfully unaware
Of the horrors
Of the next world
Where people dream of what we have
And take for granted.

Roisin Callanan (16)
The Douay Martyrs School, Ickenham

I Have A Dream

I dream every evening
Some are spectacular, while others are not
But one I had the other day
Was stuck in my mind like glue sticks to paper
If I was to tell you
If I was to even think that
My dreams will be crushed
And also me to think of that.

I dream every evening
Of what I might become
A doctor, a lawyer, I don't think that's for me.
A teacher, a binman, are you crazy?
A vet is what I want to be
People may laugh
People may drag me down
But what they think doesn't affect my self-determination
That is my dream.

I dream every evening
Now what is your dream?

Natasha Landy (15)
The Douay Martyrs School, Ickenham

The Mediterranean Dream

Standing on the beautiful beach,
Watching the crystal-clear wave
Crash in on the magnificent Mediterranean shore
Admiring the beauty that it gave.

Lying under the precious palm trees,
Gazing at the staggering sunset
Dozing off along with the gentle breeze
Later waking up, perplexed . . .

Back to algebra.

Risa Quadros (15)
The Douay Martyrs School, Ickenham

The Rude Awakening

I had a dream last night
It wasn't a good one
I dreamt no one liked me
The dream was that I was being bullied

They would laugh,
They would point,
And shout things at me

I started to cry,
What would make the pain go away?
I decided to hurt myself,
But that still didn't make it fade

They would laugh,
They would point
And shout things at me

I woke up with a fright
And thought, *it was only a dream!*
I went to school that very same day
Realising that my dream was reality.

Megan Halligan (15)
The Douay Martyrs School, Ickenham

When I Grow Up

When you grow up
What do you wanna be?
Do you wanna be holding a cup of tea?
Do you wanna be in Fame
When every single person knows your name?

Do you wanna be a model?
You may be getting loads of cuddles
If you wanna own a pub
Or even maybe a club

Do you want to be a manager?
You may be making loads of money
Why don't you just do it for Sonny?

Think about who you wanna be
Do you want to become a teacher?
You may become a preacher.

So whatever you want to be
Just go out and flee
'Cause dreams do come true!

Bethan Notley-Jones (13)
The Douay Martyrs School, Ickenham

I Have A Dream

I hope to be really successful,
Just like any other kid
Something big and well known
But nothing far too stressful.

To be an actress is my aim,
To be in theatres, films and on TV
Walking around on the red carpet,
My fans going insane.

I've tried too hard to achieve my dream,
Looking for auditions on the Internet
I'm like a photographer looking for their perfect picture
Hoping and dreaming the opportunity will come to me.

I have a dream,
To be successful
Aim high and achieve my targets
I have a dream.

Do you have one?

Milen Ghebremichael (13)
The Douay Martyrs School, Ickenham

Angel In My Dream

They say move on, where does she go?
Every day she wonders why
Why was he stolen and taken to the sky?
No chance, no time to say goodbye.
Left alone in the world to lie
Lie and dream, why?

Darkness falls and I can fly
So I go to see my angel in the sky
Smiling, you carry me down memory lane
I'm with you, I am me again
Happy and loved, no sadness, no pain.
Daylight breaks, left again she faces the rain.

They say he's gone, but they can't know.
Why every night she can see his halo
For she will not let go
Left alone in her world to lie
Lie and dream, why did you die?

Stephanie Beaver (16)
The Douay Martyrs School, Ickenham

The Fairy Tale

The difference between a boy and girl
Apart from the obvious traits
Is her ability to wish her life away
And dream of marrying someone as rich as Bill Gates.

To be hailed like a princess, respected by all
With a face radiant and bright
To succeed in singing, dancing and acting
Winning five Oscars all in one night.

To enjoy the stardom, the press and the fame
Wear Gucci, Chanel and Dior
Then along rides Prince Charming on his noble steed
Married me for evermore.

But while we're away in our own perfect worlds
Time is still ticking away
When reality hits it's hard to accept
That we're old, wrinkly and grey.

Katy Little (16)
The Douay Martyrs School, Ickenham

It All Comes Down To . . .

Life's complexities stood still, for a moment
Just a moment
People were running as free as the words on this page
Never experiencing discomfort, betrayal or rage
Everyone's desires were fulfilled
The grief from death was concealed.

Life's complexities stood still, for a moment
One short moment
The school bell rings a deafening shattering
A true awakening
I was disrupted from my dream . . .
'Oi Derwinne. For lunch today it's strawberries and cream!'

Derwinne Carlos (15)
The Douay Martyrs School, Ickenham

Daydreamer

Come into my mind,
And look around,
You'll only hear the
Same old sound.

The sound that has
Always been with me
The sound of my dreams
That want to be set free.

I dream to live with no regrets
To marry Nick Jonas
And if I work for Heat magazine
That would be a bonus.

To get the most out of life
And go to university
To inspire everyone else
And visit every city.

Betsi Burch (13)
The Douay Martyrs School, Ickenham

I Have A Dream

I have a dream
Which I believe in,
Even though no one else does.
I'm tired of getting nowhere.
I'm scared of failure,
Of being on my own.
I'm even more scared of success,
Of having everything.
Then in a flash . . .
Nothing.
That's why I have a dream
Which I believe in.

Pooja Sharma (14)
The Douay Martyrs School, Ickenham

The Disappearing Act

I had a dream last year
That my aunty would survive
She had cancer. It spread
Like bees in a hive.

I had a dream last month
My previous one now shattered
That I would meet my aunty again
Now this one is scattered.

I had a dream last week
That my heart would stop aching
But even when I try
I am obviously faking.

So, I have a dream today
That cancer will disappear
And I will help along the way
And everyone will cheer!

Amisha Raniga (16)
The Douay Martyrs School, Ickenham

Dreams

When we enter our dreams
We enter a world of our own
Dreams let us climb the highest mountain
They let us swim the deepest seas

In your dreams you wish and become
In your dreams you believe and see
In this magical world of your own
You can do anything

They can last a few minutes
But live through a lifetime
They can scare you to death
Or just put you in hysterics

Dreams are the things that go bump in the night
Dreams are the things that scare and glare
Dreams are the things that whisper in your ear
Dreams are the things that catch you off guard.

James Hester (15)
The Douay Martyrs School, Ickenham

I Have A Dream

I have a dream,
A simple dream,
I want to be . . . a dancer.

I want to be successful,
In the big, real world,
More successful than the elephant act at a circus,
But I don't aspire to be famous,
Just to have fun . . .

Although the fame would be nice,
But not being able to go anywhere,
Without being stalked
Like a leopard hunting its prey.

I try hard to accomplish my goals,
Getting closer and closer.
But all the while it gets harder and harder . . .
That's my simple dream.

Megan Finch (13)
The Douay Martyrs School, Ickenham

I Have A Dream

Staring out at a sea of umbrellas,
I see people hurrying around outside,
Dashing in the darkness and jumping over puddles,
Ahead I see twinkling red lights for miles,
Lines of cars fighting for space,
They are on an endless journey on an endless road,
I close my eyes and let my mind run away,
To a brightness and calmness, another world,
I am peaceful,
I can feel the sun on my skin,
And hear the sound of gentle waves,
Ahead of me is a carpet of golden sand, untouched,
An endless road,
I am dreaming,
My eyes open,
I rise from my chair, leave the bus and continue my journey,
My dream stays with me.

Hannah Eddery (15)
The Douay Martyrs School, Ickenham

I Have A Dream

I have a dream that one day the world will be perfect,
Where we'll have to sacrifice some things but it will be worth it!
Where every child can go to school; no matter how poor,
And everyone in the Third World countries has a reason to live for.

I have a dream that one day I will make it big as a dancer!
Where no one gets ill or dies; no such thing as cancer.
Where every morning there is a blanket of snow instead of a road;
Where no animal goes extinct and there's such a thing as superheroes.

I have a dream that one day there will be no fear;
And music and good things are the only things we can hear.
Everyone as happy as a clown!
The queen lives like one of us and has no crown.

I have a dream that one day, that can all happen . . . can it?

Mia Evans (13)
The Douay Martyrs School, Ickenham

Dreams

Dreams can come true
If you fight like a tiger
And don't let anyone stop you.

Be your own
And reach for your goal
Because your dream is what you want
Why don't you go for it?

If you want to be a horse rider
Run like the wind
You'll be Bullseye in 'Toy Story'
And you might just win!

So go on and get it
'Cause dreams can come true!

Roshni Solanki (13)
The Douay Martyrs School, Ickenham

Dreams

Every night I go to bed, hoping all I can picture is an empty void,
The thought of falling back into the haunting habitual dream
Is too much to bear,
The dream absorbs all my anxieties and fears and condenses them
into a realistic scene,
And the realism of this scene tortures me,
The possibility of this dream becoming fruition is too
Much to endure,
How can I wish that I could start again; picture a blank canvas
And create an idyllic scene,
Soft ocean waves that grace the shore, the sun's rays beaming off
the crystal-blue water,
But the background colours are too grey and black,
Too hard to erase,
Will the scene ever change?

James Griffin (17)
The Douay Martyrs School, Ickenham

My Dream

I had a dream, a dream of being on that pitch
Playing with those people
Of being the best!

Hearing the roar of the crowd
Coming out of the tunnel
With the fireworks blasting
Holding the rose for the first time

Singing the anthem
So many great people have done before me
Hearing the whistle blow
With the game won

Being on top of the world as though I was flying
The games won once again.

Patrick Nash (13)
The Douay Martyrs School, Ickenham

I Have A Dream

28th August 1963
I remember it clearly as though it was yesterday
Washington DC was flooded with people from all nations
They had come to hear Martin Luther King's inspirational words
                                                    and wisdom.
White men, black men, side by side, standing together
United and fighting for civil rights, they carried hopes on their shoulders
Of a new society and the chance of freedom
Hope glistened in my eyes as I listened carefully to the speech,
I wished I could capture that moment and keep it forever
It was like a shooting star, a spectacular moment in time.
I will never forget that day, especially the words
'I have a dream,' they still burn brightly in my heart,
I dream of a world where there is no longer a shield of hate between us
A world that one day could be a reality, not just a dream.

Amber Goonesekera (14)
The Douay Martyrs School, Ickenham

I Have A Dream

A dream is an idea
That came up in your head

A dream is a belief
Thought up while in bed

A dream may be lifelong
So never give up hope

A dream is an escape
Allowing you to hope

A dream is a dream
So should never die

For one day that dream
Could become reality.

Daniel Haras-Gummer (15)
The Douay Martyrs School, Ickenham

Young Writers Information

We hope you have enjoyed reading this book - and that you will continue to enjoy it in the coming years.

If you like reading and writing poetry drop us a line, or give us a call, and we'll send you a free information pack.

Alternatively if you would like to order further copies of this book or any of our other titles, then please give us a call or log onto our website at www.youngwriters.co.uk

Young Writers Information
Remus House
Coltsfoot Drive
Peterborough
PE2 9JX
(01733) 890066